WHAT'S THE IS

FAKE NEWS

TOM JACKSON • CRISTINA GUITIAN

Quarto is the authority on a wide range of topics.

Quarto educates, entertains and enriches the lives of our readers—enthusiasts and lovers of hands-on living.

www.quartoknows.com

MIX
Paper from
responsible sources
FSC® C008047

Author: Tom Jackson
Illustrator: Cristina Guitian
Designer: Mike Henson
Editors: Claire Watts and Ellie Brough
Consultant: Ellie Levenson
Creative Director: Malena Stojic
Publisher: Maxime Boucknooghe

This edition first published in 2020 by QEB Publishing,
an imprint of The Quarto Group.
26391 Crown Valley Parkway, Suite 220
Mission Viejo, CA 92691, USA
T: +1 949 380 7510
F: +1 949 380 7575
www.QuartoKnows.com

A CIP record for this book is available from the Library of Congress.

ISBN 978 0 7112 5034 5

Manufactured in Gunagdong, China
CC062020

9 8 7 6 5 4 3 2 1

CONTENTS

AUTHOR'S NOTE

WHAT'S THE ISSUE WITH FAKE NEWS?

The news media is very powerful. Without it we would not know much about what is going on in the world, and whatever we did know would be old news already. But there are many people around today warning us that the news is fake and it is being made up to hide the truth or trick us. If you are confused by fake news then you are not alone—fake news is designed to cause confusion. I can't tell you what's real, but I can tell you what I know and set out what's what and who's who.

THEN IT'S UP TO YOU TO MAKE AN INFORMED OPINION.

I'll show you how humans have always made up stories to explain, entertain, and innovate. We'll see that although fake news seems like a recent invention, it's actually nothing new. We'll explore how news can become faked in different ways and for different reasons. It's complicated, but you are going to need to know all this to be able to figure out what news is true and what news is not. It's not easy as often there is no simple answer.

SO WHAT DO YOU THINK?
WHAT DO YOUR FRIENDS THINK?
WHAT DO YOUR TEACHERS THINK?
WHAT DO YOUR PARENTS THINK?

Everyone and anyone can have an opinion, but not everyone's opinion is fully informed. With this book you'll have the knowledge to back up your arguments.

OPINIONS MATTER, SO WHAT WILL YOURS BE?

WHAT'S TRUTH GOT TO DO WITH IT?

Everything in this book is the truth, the whole truth, and nothing but the truth. Ah, I've done it already. I've lied. Sorry. There is going to be a whole lot of falsehood as well as truth in here. We will explore the ideas around communication and the news media, as well as why people make up fake news stories and how to spot them. Fake news is nothing new. The Roman emperors used it to try to discredit their rivals, and politicians used to lie about each other much more than they would ever do now. So why are you and I here in this book? Read on—you won't be disappointed.

POST-TRUTH

Some people have a rather gloomy outlook. They say we are living in a "post-truth" world, where being informed and expert in a subject is no longer important. In addition, it seems we no longer all need to agree on what is true and what is false—we can believe whatever suits us. If we don't like the facts we can simply adopt "alternative facts." Is that even possible? As we'll explore later, the way we use information has changed in the last few years. The most important thing now appears to be our opinion, even if it's on matters we don't really know anything about.

DEEP STATE

Post-truth has gone so far that some people believe that we are controlled by a "deep state," or "state within a state." Some people think that the politicians and mainstream media are all in it together to distract us from the fact that our votes don't mean anything any more. This is an idea that a much greater number of people are prepared to accept now, compared to a few years ago. Fake news, conspiracy theories, and straightforward lies are being used to turn sections of society against another. What can we do about that? Read on to find out.

WHAT'S WHAT?

THE MEDIA

It is the job of the media to keep us informed about what is going on in the world. The media is made up of many types of news medium, such as newspapers, magazines, TV, radio, online news sites, and social media. The news media has a difficult job. It needs to inform and educate us about complex subjects but keep us entertained at the same time. Over time, the news media has had to alter the way it works, and it is still changing as we increasingly communicate online.

THE CONSEQUENCES OF SPEECH

We should all be blessed with the freedom of speech and, in many places in the world, people can say more or less whatever they want. However, **freedom of speech** doesn't give us freedom from the consequences of what we say. Spreading false information and fake news has consequences that we are only just beginning to fully understand. Who gets to decide what is true and what is false anyway?

WHAT IS FAKE NEWS?

How should we define fake news? Is it anything that turns out to be false—even if it was reported by mistake? Is it news that promotes one idea unfairly over another? Or is it only news reports that have been deliberately created to stir up trouble?

THE EVOLUTION OF SPEECH

We humans are the only animals that use language. That is to say we do not simply alert each other with calls of a particular sound. Instead we create meaning by constructing sentences with interchangeable words. (I did that just then.) So why did humans develop this extraordinary ability and how does it make us different from our animal relatives?

Many things set humans apart from other animals: tools, hands, big brains...but speech may be the most important of all. Most conversations take place between two or three people and sometimes what is said is about other people who aren't present. From the earliest human societies, spreading rumors and telling lies was a powerful tool for causing conflicts—and preventing them as well. Nothing much has changed, has it?

SOCIAL GLUE

Humans evolved from apes who lived in the lush forests where our nearest relatives, the chimpanzees, still live. Chimps live in groups of about 50 who work together to find food and secure territory. When early humans left the forests for Africa's grasslands, they began to live in groups about three times this size. (Even today most people can easily remember the names and faces of 150 people.) Chimps build personal relationships by sitting quietly and grooming each other. That's not really possible in a group of 150, so instead we developed talking as a way to maintain good relations.

INFORMATION EXCHANGE

Let's look at the kinds of information exchanged in typical conversations. Imagine a couple of early humans are chatting:

Fact: Our leader was killed by a boar during a hunt last night.

Lie: The new leader could have saved him but actually helped the boar kill him.

Little lie: Our leader was a very good hunter.

Exaggeration: The boar was the size of a bear!

Plan: On the next hunt we will kill that boar so it doesn't hurt anyone else.

Prediction: I think our new leader will be the one to do that.

Fantasy: Our leader's spirit is now in all boars.

Opinion: I think hunting is too dangerous. Let's not do it any more.

WHAT'S WHAT?

CELEBRITY

We live in much bigger social groups today than prehistoric people did. City dwellers may live in groups of a million or more and most are total strangers. However, we can still establish a common link by gossiping about celebrities. A celebrity—be they an athlete, actor or social media star—is someone we might never meet in person, yet know all about them.

TEACHING TOOL

As with many complex features, speech probably didn't evolve for one reason alone. The parts of the brain used for controlling speech and understanding language are very close to the regions we use when crafting something with our hands, such as whittling wood or hammering a rock into an axe head. This suggests that speech evolved to help us communicate complex ideas—how to make a flint axe, for example.

IMAGINE

It has been argued that the whole of human civilization arises from speech. It would be more precise to say it comes from learning to lie. Lying requires you to imagine something that didn't happen, though it might be inspired by true events. It's a short jump to imagining things that might happen in the future, and so you start to plan. How about dreaming up something that has never happened? Now you are inventing and innovating. What will you think of next?

TRANSLATION PARADOX

When you learn another language, you learn how to translate from the words of your language to the new one. All languages can be translated from one to the other, including going from today's languages to ones used in the past. But at some point there was just a single first language. Back then we couldn't use another language to explain the meaning of each word. Instead the meaning of language was agreed without using words at all!

To lie and cheat, you need to have a "theory of mind." This is the understanding that the contents of your mind are different from the contents of everyone else's. Infants haven't figured this out yet. They think what they know, see, and hear, is what everyone else knows, sees, and hears as well. That's why hide and seek is no fun for very little kids. They just cover their eyes because if they can't see you, they believe you can't see them.

EMOTIONAL TRUTH

A speaker conveys emotions through a tone of voice and visual signals, such as facial expressions. The function of emotions is complex: fear and anger prepare us for danger, while sadness and happiness encourage friends to support us. Faking emotions is hard to do well, thanks in part to the "sclera" or white of the eye. The sclera helps us see where someone is looking, and if they are lying or faking an emotion their "shifty eyes" often give it away.

It is not really possible for animals to be dishonest. In biology, an honest signal is one that puts the signaller at a disadvantage. For example, a meerkat sounds the alarm to warn the rest of the mob about an eagle, but it draws the eagle's attention, putting itself at risk. It would not fake this alarm. Animals, however, are master deceivers. They play dead to deter predators, puff themselves up to appear more threatening, and even mimic entirely different animals to fool each other.

WHO'S WHO?

NOAM CHOMSKY

This American linguist made his name in the 1960s when he proposed that human language used a basic structure he called the "universal grammar." Chomsky proposed that this structure was hardwired into the brain and not learned by listening to adults. Not everyone agrees with this idea, but Chomsky said it explained how children acquire words and meanings really fast.

WHAT IF HUMANS COULDN'T LIE?

Is there ever a good lie? Would it be better to always be honest? What would that be like? Our ability to lie and fake things comes from being able to imagine alternative realities. If we were unable to lie, would we also be unable to innovate? Would it be worth it?

THE INVENTION OF WRITING

Writing is a remarkable invention that allows my mind to connect to yours. It can be used to express thoughts and feelings that are not always clear in the spoken word. You, the reader, see a reflection of your own thoughts and feelings in those words. Just as importantly, writing is a record of facts and ideas that can outlive the writer and be spread around the world and down the ages. What shall we write about?

The significance of symbols is illustrated by the seals of the Indus Valley civilization which existed 7,500 years ago in what is now Pakistan. These seals were small blocks of carved soapstone showing impressive creatures and monsters. Each unique symbol represented a family and was printed on goods to show ownership and **authenticity**. They were the autograph or encryption key of their day.

PROTO-WRITING

Writing was invented in the Middle East about 5,000 years ago in a region once known as Mesopotamia, where the first cities were built. But for thousands of years before that, people were making marks known as "proto-writing." These were symbols that helped them remember things or represented significant concepts or events. We don't know what all these ancient symbols mean, but they eventually evolved into the letters you are reading now.

HIEROGLYPHS

In hieroglyphics, the picture-based writing system used by the ancient Egyptians, an image of a cat means "cat" and a reed image means "reed." The system was used in various forms until 500 CE. Gradually, the symbols began to be used to represent entire words or phrases. Some hieroglyphs operated as "phonemes," or letter sounds, in the same way most alphabets work today.

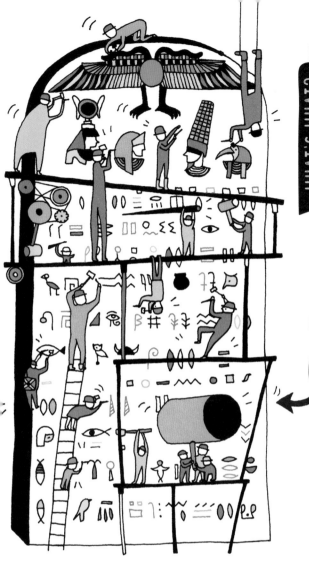

ROSETTA STONE

The art of reading hieroglyphics had long been lost until, in 1799, Napoleon Bonaparte's army found the Rosetta Stone, a 2,000-year-old slab engraved with writing. One section of the text was Ancient Greek, which was still read then; another section was in demotic, an Egyptian alphabet similar to Greek; and the top part was in hieroglyphics. When experts realized that each text was almost identical in meaning they were able to work out how to read hieroglyphics.

CUNEIFORM

Before hieroglyphics there was the Mesopotamian writing system called 'cuneiform'. This was written by making marks in wet clay with a wedge-shaped reed. These marks also started out as simple pictures of animals and other goods. This evolved into more stylized symbols which were then split into letters. Although cuneiform was the dominant writing for 3,000 years it has no descendent writing systems today.

Cuneiform probably arose from a way of accounting for livestock that involved marking notches on a stick. Simple tally marks recording each goat developed into more complex symbols for several goats, and once transferred to wet clay, the symbols continued to develop to represent words. Writing numbers predates writing words. The oldest tally sticks are 40,000 years old! They may have had a mathematical purpose beyond simply recording numbers, but that is another story.

Important people used to set the deeds they were most proud of in stone—literally. They carved writing into ceremonial columns called "steles," like the Rosetta Stone. These impressive texts were usually accounts of achievements or long lists of possessions. But should we believe these reports? They were made to boost the standing of a great leader, so the facts might have been tweaked to put them in the best light.

ALPHABETS

The Latin script used in most countries today, plus the Greek, Cyrillic, Arabic, and numerous Asian alphabets, all arose from the Phoenician alphabet. This appeared in what is now Lebanon about 3,000 years ago. It was inspired by shapes of hieroglyphs but used letters to represent sounds and put them together to make words. The idea appears to have caught on!

MAKING A RECORD

Not all ancient writing is boasting; some records rules and systems of justice. Such is the power of the written word that these texts laid the foundation of today's laws and government. One of the first of these texts was the Code of Hammurabi, a list of laws from Babylon, which we can read even though it was written 3,750 years ago. It explains how people should trade and make agreements and lists punishments for various crimes.

WHAT'S WHAT?

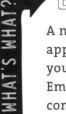

EMOJIS

A new way of writing has appeared in recent years, and you're probably already an expert. Emojis work like hieroglyphs, communicating meaning as symbols. Emojis first appeared in Japan in 1999, when telephone engineer Shigetaka Kunitz wanted a way of sending short messages via mobile phone. There are now nearly 3,000 emojis, but the most used ones indicate emotion. Without the facial expressions and tone of voice that add emotion to spoken conversation, it's easy to misinterpret what someone has written. An emoji makes all the difference.

ARE WRITTEN WORDS MORE IMPORTANT THAN SPOKEN ONES?

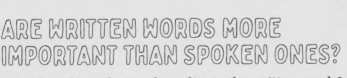

There has always been a formality to the written word. Is it right to think that if someone wrote words down they must be significant—and are more likely to be true? Does relying too much on the written word mean that we miss all kinds of ideas and opinions?

MYTHS AND MEANING

Ancient **myths** still exist across the world hundreds or thousands of years after they were first written down. Who hasn't heard of the Trojan Horse or Noah and the Flood? But are any of them remotely true? They are "myths," which are **fictional** accounts of significant events in the distant past of a country or culture. As a record of the past, they are totally fake news, but the information they contain about where we come from is still useful.

MYTHOS AND LOGOS

Experts divide knowledge into two types: the "mythos" and the "logos." The logos are things that can be verified by reason or facts, such as the succession of rulers, winners of wars, and scientific laws. The mythos is the understanding of the world based on the stories of heroes and monsters. Modern society is packed full of logos, but our culture emerged over millions of years from primitive societies with no logos at all. The mythos fills the gap between these two states; it arises from our earliest attempts to make sense of our emotions, fears, and appetites for life.

CREATION MYTHS

Every culture has its own creation myth to explain how the universe was formed. The major world religions, which originated from the Middle East and south Asia, say that the Universe arose from nothingness or chaos by introducing order and light. The Kuba people of central Africa describe how their god vomited out the Sun, Moon, and Earth! The creation myths of northern Europe believe the universe emerged from a parent being, while the myths of north Asian and American cultures often involve beings who awoke at the beginning of time to build the world.

Many myths and **legends** involve killing a monster. Saint George famously slew a dragon, while Hercules killed the Hydra, a beast that could kill you with its breath! We could explain these away: George probably killed a man-eating crocodile menacing a town in North Africa, while the Hydra represented a volcanic cave filled with toxic gas. The killing of a terrifying monster appears in many stories because it represents a basic fear, dating back to when we were preyed upon by lions and hyenas.

WHO'S WHO?

HOMER

The most famous stories of Greek mythology are said to have been written 3,000 years ago by a blind poet named Homer. He wrote two long books called the *Iliad* and the *Odyssey*. However, that is probably an early version of fake news. There's no evidence that Homer ever lived, and it is more likely that Homer's writings are made up of ancient stories that were told by performing poets and only written down much later.

FACT AND FICTION

As well as making great yarns, there may be a link to reality in some myths. In the story of the Trojan Horse, the Greeks sent an enormous wooden horse into the city of Troy as a gift. During the night, Greek soldiers climbed out of the horse and defeated the city. Doesn't sound very likely, does it? But the horse was a symbol of Poseidon, god of the sea and of earthquakes. So perhaps the Greeks didn't beat Troy using a wooden horse, but an earthquake damaged the city, leaving the Trojans vulnerable to attack.

Fantastic fictional fakes, myths, and folk tales often tell of things that can't be explained by science. When magic is performed by a divine power, this is called a "miracle." A good example of a miracle is a statue that cries tears. This seems impossible, so it must be a sign of divine power. But miracles like water trickling from a statue's eye aren't necessarily impossible—just very unlikely—a one-in-a-million chance, perhaps. According to the mathematical law of Truly Large Numbers, a one-in-a-million event, like a crying statue, will happen every month, so miracles might actually be quite common.

FAIRY TALES

Once upon a time, people would entertain each other with stories of everyday folk— plus magical animals, witches, and goblins. Such tales were told aloud across the world, before being written down by collectors, like the Brothers Grimm. Since then, fairy tales have been retold as movie animations, books, ballets, and plays—often reshaped to suit a modern audience. Fairy tales draw on themes that have always been important, such as fear of the unknown, the process of growing up, betrayal, greed, and love.

MORALITY TALES

Much of ancient mythology is also fiction with a message. Take the story of the inventor Daedalus. Daedalus built wings for himself and his son, Icarus, from feathers and wax. Daedalus warned Icarus not to fly too high, but his son ignored him and soared like a god through the sky. The Sun's rays melted the wax holding the feathers in place, and Icarus plummeted into the sea. This is obviously untrue, but the message is clear— do not try to imitate the gods.

Stories are older than writing. They were told by traveling performers, known as "bards" or "minstrels." As well as stories, bards sang songs, put on plays, and spread news. With each telling, a story might change slightly. This is why there are so many overlapping folk tales that have similar characters or themes. However, when news is retold like this, the truth of events becomes obscured by frequent retellings by different people. As any seasoned performer will agree, we should never let the truth get in the way of a good story.

WHAT'S WHAT?

URBAN LEGEND

Legends are slightly different than myths—they are said to have taken place in history, rather than in a time before humans existed. Robin Hood and King Arthur are both legendary figures. "Urban legends" created today are scary or funny stories or quirky facts. They spread through society, evolving with each retelling. Have you heard that eating apple seeds will make a tree grow in your stomach? Completely fake!

IS FAKING A STORY ALWAYS A BAD THING?

Everyone loves a story. How much of a true story should actually be true and how much can be made up—and how do you tell the difference? Should we assume all stories are fake?

RECORDING HISTORY

History is the story of past events. Histories are true stories but they still have a writer who choses how to tell them. How reliable are these stories, and does it matter? History records the big stuff, like the foundation of countries and governments, wars, and people who changed the world. Historians also show us what everyday life was like in the past. They say that those who ignore history are doomed to repeat it, so pay attention!

RETURN TO THE SOURCE

Historians are like detectives—they build the history of the past by collecting clues. Sources, such as written materials, are useful although they too have an author so must be treated with some skepticism. Other sources include ruined buildings, tools, and even ancient garbage dumps. Taken together these sources build a picture that exposes fakery and reinforces facts. These analytical skills could be used to expose fake news.

Not all historical sources are equal. Some outrank others for their power to tell us about the past. A **primary source** is the best. It is an original record created at the time in question, such as an account of a tribal chief surrendering to an invading king written by a soldier who was there.
A **secondary source** is a text that comments on a primary source. For example, it might mention the chief's surrender while discussing the king's methods to expand his kingdom.
A **tertiary source** is a reference book covering the topic—a bit like this one.

CHRONICLES

Among the best primary sources are chronicles. These are records of events, written as they occur. Chronicles, also known as "sagas" or "annals," provide a list of events in time order. They may include lists of festivals or the deaths of priests and leaders, as well as bigger events like wars and natural disasters. Several chronicles overlapping in time can confirm the timing of events, or correct mistakes, and could be combined to create one history of the world!

WHAT'S WHAT?

DOMESDAY BOOK

Pronounced "doomsday," this is one of the most famous books in English history. It was a record of just about everything in England in 1086, twenty years after the country had been taken over by the Norman king William the Conqueror. It is a survey of landowners, farms, mills, and houses. William was not interested in fake news; he needed to know facts. If it was not in the *Domesday Book*, it did not exist.

MAKING COPIES

By the sixth century, chronicles and other important writings were held in handmade books. The books were often "illuminated"—filled with intricate colored artworks. To speed up the copying process and to reduce errors, scribes often specialized in reproducing a single page, working in large teams to produce each book. It doesn't sound like much fun, but these people were the technology geeks of their day!

IS HISTORY WRITTEN BY THE WINNERS?

The old saying goes that history is written by the victors. It means that the people in charge get to record what happened—and make themselves look good and their enemies look bad. Does that mean history is just old fake news?

MAKING PICTURES

It is true what they say—"a picture speaks a thousand words." Sight is our primary sense, and we can collect a lot of information just by looking. Unlike animals, humans create representations of what we see and imagine as pictures. These images have the power to convey a lot of meaning. However, who's to say what that meaning is? Sometimes, not even the artist is sure.

The retina of the eye which collects light is itself a two-dimensional surface. Our visual perception of three dimensions, where distant objects appear farther away than near ones, is created by our brains, mostly by comparing the slight differences in view from either eye. Animals that have side-facing eyes, like a chicken or cow, cannot see depth and distance in the same way humans and cats can.

SYMBOLIC ART

We've never stopped making images on walls, from the detailed friezes on the walls of ancient Egyptian and Mesopotamian tombs to today's street art. Tomb images are painted on plaster or carved in stone. Ancient drawings had a two-dimensional look and took a symbolic approach to representing real things, based on the number and size of images. For example, the power of the king or pharaoh was shown by making him a giant compared to ordinary people.

CAVE PAINTINGS

Humans are thought to have been around for almost 200,000 years, living in Africa until about 70,000 years ago. For most of that time, we did not create pictures. But about 50,000 years ago, paintings of animals and hunters appeared. Images painted on the walls of deep caves have survived until now, but prehistoric artists probably painted them elsewhere too. Were these scenes of great hunts records of what happened? Or were we even faking the news back then?

Our eyes see all the colors of the rainbow when we look at the natural world, but pictures are restricted by the chemical pigments used to color paints and inks. Ancient artists relied on chalk and charcoal and rusty browns of powered metal ores. **Medieval** chemists added more vibrant pigments of gold, blue, and green, from concoctions of urine and leaves or using chemicals we now know are poisonous, such as arsenic, mercury, and even uranium.

WHO'S WHO?

OLD MASTERS

The top painters working before the 1800s are known as "Old Masters." Their art pre-dates photography and copying technology, so they were making the most accurate versions of reality possible at the time. Even though we can make perfect copies of these pictures and make truer likenesses of the subjects they show, the Old Masters' sketches and paintings are highly valued because of their amazing skill.

GETTING THINGS IN PERSPECTIVE

In the 1400s, Italian painters began to use new technologies like glass mirrors, lenses, and advances in mathematics to try to create paintings that looked three-dimensional. The result was to add **perspective** so pictures looked more like the way our eyes see the world. This new way of making images transformed art. Once artists learned to represent real things accurately, they soon began creating unreal things—such as past events or mythical scenes—in the same way.

PORTRAITS

Human visual perception is finely tuned to look at faces—to spot minute differences and detect signs of emotion, faked or otherwise. The job of a portrait painter was not just to create a true likeness of their subject but also convey something about them. This involved surrounding people with their valued possessions or placing them overlooking their land or in a work setting. These pictures may be the only record of how a person looked. Can we trust what we see?

HIDDEN MEANING

The Old Masters used a technique called "allegory" to inject deeper meanings into their pictures. One of the most famous paintings in the world, *The Creation of Adam* by Michelangelo, shows the first human touching the hand of God. A closer look reveals that God and the nymphs around him are arranged in the shape of the human brain. When it was painted in 1512, this was a subversive subject because studying human anatomy was frowned upon by the religious authorities, and Michelangelo had painted the picture for the Pope himself!

Portraits were not simply vanity projects. Miniaturists specialized in creating small pictures of loved ones for people to carry on their travels. Portraits were also a primitive form of ID. Henry VIII asked the artist Hans Holbein the Younger to capture the looks of Anne of Cleves, so he could decide if he wanted to marry her. Henry was impressed with what he saw, but when Anne arrived in England for the wedding, he accused Holbein of faking the portrait.

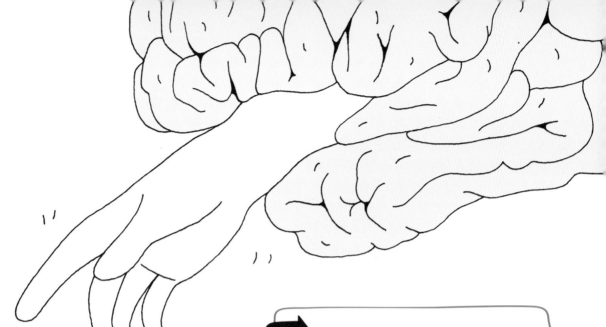

FORGERIES

It's possible to make near perfect copies of any picture. Expert artists use the same paints and techniques as the Old Masters to copy their work. Owners of old paintings may have copies made to put on display because the real painting is too valuable to hang in public. Criminals also try to sell unofficial copies—called "forgeries"—or swap them for the real thing without anyone noticing. But hang on, the fake and the original look identical (except in age). Why is the fake one worth less?

WHAT'S WHAT?

ABSTRACT ART

By the twentieth century, some painters stopped trying to create recognizable images of real things. Instead they painted abstract art made up of shapes, colors, and textures. Abstract art grew from a time when humans were remaking the world into whatever they wanted by building megacities, designing complex machines and fighting terrible wars. Everyday life was becoming ever more unreal and so was the art.

IS IT BETTER FOR A PICTURE TO HAVE A HIDDEN MEANING?

There is more than one way to appreciate a painting. You can marvel at its colors and the skill with which it was produced and take in the people and places it shows us. But is that enough? Did the artist want to tell us more?

THE INVENTION OF PRINTING

If writing was the first important communication technology, then the printing press was the second. Before this, hand-written books and hand-painted pictures could contain important truths or mischievous lies, but few people ever saw or heard about them. Printing made it possible to make copies of these works quickly and cheaply, for more people. Spreading ideas suddenly got a lot easier.

THE PRESS

The printing press gets its name because early machines were based on a device for pressing grapes to make wine. A flat plate was lowered by a screw to crush grapes or press down on paper. The paper was pressed against a shape coated in ink and that shape appeared on the paper. In the 1440s, a German metalworker named Johannes Gutenberg devised a way of making metal lettering, or "type." It could be set in any order to spell out any text and printed over and over again.

Guess what? The fact that Gutenberg invented printing is fake news. The technology was developed in China at least 1,400 years before. Chinese printers first used a system where shapes were carved into wood, but this took longer than writing so it didn't work as a fast copying method. Later they used type made from pottery and wood. By the eleventh century, Korean printers were using metal type. The trouble was Chinese and Korean text required thousands of characters, which made printing like this very complex.

MOVEABLE TYPE

Gutenberg developed a system for creating coins in a way to make molds for letters. The type is called "moveable," because the individual letters could be arranged into one text and then rearranged to spell out new text. Arranging the type was the job of the typesetter. They kept type in two boxes, or "cases." The small letters which were used most were kept in the lower case and the capitals were in the upper case. See what happened there?

WHAT'S WHAT?

GUTENBERG'S BIBLE

The first book ever printed is the Gutenberg Bible from 1455. It took three years for Gutenberg to produce 180 copies, which was still much faster than doing it by hand. He even added colors by running pages through the press several times with different inks on each pass.

PUBLISHING

By the 1500s, there were already several thousand printed books across Europe. Printing was still expensive and so a new kind of businessperson appeared: the publisher. The publisher pays for an author's book to be printed, and in exchange, they keep some of the money whenever a book is sold. Printing created a new industry that sold stories and information. Where would that lead?

WHAT WOULD YOU PUBLISH?

This is your big chance to get into print. What would you do with it? You could write a story that talks to people's emotions. You could set out your ideas for making the world better. Or why not make up some funny lies about an enemy? Which will be the most successful?

It takes time to make a book, even today – this one has taken an entire team of people working for several months. (You're welcome!) We've built it to last, with words and pictures that will be worth looking at for years to come. However, in the seventeenth century, a new kind of printed publication began to develop that was only interesting for a short amount of time. After that you threw it away and bought another. It's the newspaper and the people that make them are called "**the press**."

OLD NEWS

Newspapers began in Germany 400 years ago. At first, they were really "news books" printed every week containing stories about the latest events. The idea was that people would pay to read news that would otherwise take days or weeks (or even years) to reach them via word of mouth. The news was mostly local, because that was all the writers knew about, but similar publications from other cities and countries steadily became a source of news from farther afield. Soon, newspapers offered a summary of national and international news.

JOHANN CAROLUS

This German publisher produced the first newspaper, called *Relation aller Fürnemmen und gedenckwürdigen Historien* (which means "Account of all distinguished and memorable stories"), in 1605 in Strasbourg. Carolus's idea of selling news caught on, and by the early 1800s newspapers were being printed in all major cities of the world.

Fake news has been a problem from the start. This was because of incompetence and mistakes—editors had fewer ways to check facts. In the late eighteenth century, George III, the English king, was so fed up with incorrect reporting about what he and his family were doing that he created the *Court Circular*. This is an official record of royal engagements that's still printed in a few British papers.

EDITORIAL PROCESS

After I finish writing this book, it will go to an editor (hi Ellie!), who will get rid of the boring bits (see, none left!) and make sure the rest makes sense. These are **editorial** decisions, and they are made on every kind of publication, including newspapers. An editor of a newspaper has different priorities when editing than a book editor does. The subjects covered are best if they have never been written about before – so the newspaper becomes their primary source. Also, the editor wants you to buy this paper, not another, so the stories have to amaze and excite or shock and scare.

PAPER OF RECORD

By the start of the twentieth century, every country had a newspaper of record, a publication that promoted itself as a truthful account of the most important news. This was a bit like an updated version of the medieval chronicle (see page 21). In fact, some are called *The Chronicle*, while others have titles like *The Times*, *The World*, or *The Post*.

JOURNALISTS

Newspapers are produced by journalists. There are three basic types: an editor, a sub-editor, and a reporter. Editors are in charge of a newspaper or a section of one. They decide which stories are printed and where they go in the paper. Before that can happen, reporters go out and find the news. They witness events, interview people, and snoop around uncovering secrets. They then write a report about what they find. Next the sub-editor reorganizes that story so it fits with all the others in the newspaper, and gives it a **headline**, or title.

MAGAZINES

Hot on the heels of newspapers came the magazine. The word "magazine" comes from an old word meaning storehouse. Magazine editors focus less on news and fill their publications with stories that a reader can dip into over several days or weeks and not feel they are outdated. Some magazines target readers with a particular interest, such as birdwatching. Others provide information about things that everyone does to some extent, such as watching TV, buying clothes, or keeping fit.

READ ALL ABOUT IT!

The first newspapers looked more like books than today's newspapers. They had smallish pages (a little bigger than this book) with the text printed in a single wide column. Then journalists began to print on bigger sheets, so newspapers measured about 3 feet across when opened. The stories were printed in narrow columns side by side. At first, the text was small to save on paper, but as printing became cheaper, sub-editors and designers were able to create more enticing front pages to get the attention (and money) of the public. Today, a paper's main story, known as the "**splash**," is chosen to have as big an impact as possible.

Journals look like magazines, but are a very different kind of publication. They're produced by academic institutions to publish the latest discoveries and breakthroughs. If you look at the page numbers, you'll see that they seem far too high. That is because when one journal ends the next one begins, so they can be bound together every year to form a single book. Journals are a record of knowledge so the contents are checked very carefully so that the readers can trust it is correct.

WHAT'S WHAT?

EXCLUSIVE!

The best way to attract attention to a newspaper is to cover a story that no other paper has. This is an "exclusive." Reporters work hard to discover something that no one else knows about, and then keep it secret until they can publish it. Editors may even make fake front covers that fool spies snooping from other newspapers.

DO YOU WRITE FAKE NEWS?

A headline needs to set out the main facts of the story and entice you to read it, all in half a dozen words. That's not easy. Try a few yourself and ask your friends which is the most interesting. How true to the facts is your best headline? Did you bend the truth to get attention?

FORMING OPINIONS

Despite the name, newspapers devote a lot of their space to stuff that isn't news—like opinion pieces. The main one is the editorial or "leader." This presents the opinion of a newspaper's editor (and its owner). It may relate to what politicians are doing or to the behavior of a public figure. It may even be trying to influence a change in the law. The person who writes the leader has a big audience and a lot of power. Who gave it to them?

To be successful, newspaper editors target their editorials at a specific group of readers. Politicians aim to represent people in the same way, but instead of selling newspapers, they're trying to convince people to vote for them. Every newspaper has a political position. Even the ones that are independent and remain unaligned with a political party have something to say.

THE FOURTH ESTATE

It was not long before people who owned and wrote newspapers began to understand their power to influence events, and even governments. In 1787, Irish politician Edmund Burke described the press as the "**Fourth Estate**." By "estate," he meant that there was an extra power at work in society; the other three were the monarch, the church, and the people. We'll see later just how powerful newspaper owners, or "press barons," can be.

DIFFERENT VIEWS

A newspaper editor also pays people to write about their opinions. These articles traditionally appear opposite the editorial and are called "op-eds." Op-ed journalists are also known as "columnists," because they get their own text column to fill. Some write about a specialized subject, such as sports, politics, or money, but others simply aim to entertain and engage the readers. Columnists focus on getting a reaction by outraging the readers or by discussing issues that concern them. In this way, a column can become a kind of performance rather than a piece of writing meant to change minds.

SATIRE

One of the jobs of journalism is to tell leaders when they are making mistakes. In ancient times, that was a risky business. If the person in power didn't like being told off, you risked being imprisoned (or worse). Traditionally, a jester or clown could get away with making fun of the king. He or she played the fool and had no power, and so could make jokes about royal errors. This ancient form of political humor is called "satire," and it is regularly used in newspapers, in columns, or in cartoons.

WHO'S WHO?

WILLIAM HOGARTH

This English artist was famous for producing satirical paintings and drawings in the eighteenth century. He employed humor and moral tales to poke fun at society. Perhaps Hogarth's most famous work is the *Rake's Progress*, a story told in eight pictures packed with details about a wealthy young man who steadily wastes his fortune and ends up going insane.

DO NEWSPAPERS AFFECT YOUR OPINIONS?

Or do you read that newspaper because the editors include things you already agree with? This is one of the most important questions in modern society. And it's a tough one. How easy would it be for me to change your opinion?

SEEING IS BELIEVING

Ten years ago, no one used the word "selfie" and twenty years ago, few people carried a camera wherever they went. Today, most of us snap pics all day long. Since its invention, photography has been a very powerful means of communication. Pictures of wars and natural disasters can spread stories around the world in minutes. People say "seeing is believing," but as soon as photos were invented people found ways to fake them.

The term photography means "drawing with light." This name is even better suited to the technology of modern digital photography. Digital cameras turn beams of light into computer code, which can be used to recreate the image using dots, or pixels, of varying color and intensity. And fakery just got a lot easier—change the code and you change the picture.

SILVER IMAGES

By the mid 1800s, various inventors had found ways to capture images using light-sensitive chemicals. The chemicals were exposed to light inside a camera (basically an artificial eye) to capture the pattern of a scene. Next, other chemicals were used to develop the pattern into a visible image. There was much room for fakery including exposing photographs twice or cutting and pasting several images together.

PHOTOJOURNALISM

Before photos, newspapers used illustrations which were etched onto a metal plate for printing. These illustrated news titles appealed to people who struggled to read. The pictures included portraits, cartoons, and reimagined versions of true-life events. Photography offered a much better view of true events, especially places of great suffering which appalled and fascinated readers.

FAMOUS FAKES

The first piece of faked photojournalism was created by Hippolyte Bayard, one of the inventors competing to create a working photographic system. When he was beaten to this goal by Louis Daguerre in the 1830s, Bayard created a fake picture showing himself drowning! One of the most famous sets of fake pictures was published in 1920. They showed two girls with tiny fairies in their garden. Despite much skepticism, no one could prove the Cottingley Fairies weren't real. In 1983, the girls, by then elderly ladies, confessed that the fairies were card cut-outs.

WHAT'S WHAT?

THE SURGEON'S PHOTO

In 1934, Colonel Robert Wilson, a surgeon in the British Army, delivered a photo to the *Daily Mail* in London after a holiday in Scotland. The picture appears to show the head and neck of a strange creature in the waters of Loch Ness. But, of course this Loch Ness Monster is fake. The head is a model stuck on top of a remote-controlled toy submarine. It was not even taken by Colonel Wilson but by a prankster who hated the *Daily Mail* and tricked them into putting the fake story on their front page.

IS SEEING BELIEVING ANY MORE?

Strangely the most ordinary photos are the hardest to fake because we are good at spotting stuff that does not look quite right. How closely do you look at photos? Would you be able to spot a fake?

CONTROLLING THE STORY

Since the 1600s, journalism has provided society with information and has helped people understand the world. However, there are other forces, such as governments, trying to control this information. Sensitive facts are removed, or "censored," from news reports. The flip side of **censorship** is "**propaganda**," or approved news, which promotes a preferred set of messages. News has been manipulated plenty of times in the past. But is it happening now?

CENSORING CENSORS

Now, don't get me wrong—censorship is not all bad and it is a necessary part of a civilized society. The age-rating system for cinema films and computer games are censorship. They protect young people from seeing graphic depictions of violence or sex that they won't fully understand. Censorship also makes it illegal to call for attacks on other people or stir up hatred of groups based on sexuality, religion, or race. However, the power of the official censorship must be balanced with freedom of speech—that's the right to say what you want. We'll be coming back to this for sure!

OFFICIAL SECRETS

Breaking censorship will always get you in trouble, but especially if you reveal official secrets. These are the pieces of information that a government decides must be hidden to keep the country and its people safe. They include things like new weapons for the military or the activities of spies. Give that stuff away and you could end up in prison, or in some countries, even put to death! However, people have discovered that official secrecy rules are being used to hide how governments break laws or make serious mistakes. Find out what they do about it on page 74.

In democratic countries, censorship is mostly controlled using laws which define what's allowed in terms of age limits and content. One form of censorship that's often being tested is personal privacy. The laws vary considerably from place to place, but individuals generally have the right to ask a judge to grant an "injunction," which blocks the publication of sensitive information. Getting injunctions can cost a lot of money, so wealthy people are able to protect their secrets more easily than everyone else.

CLEANING HISTORY

Joseph Stalin ruled the Soviet Union, a communist empire that once spread from Eastern Europe to the Asian Pacific, from 1927 to 1953. To keep power, he killed any member of the government who disagreed with him. He then removed evidence of them from all official documents in a process called "sanitization." If a photo contained one of Stalin's ex-advisers, it was withdrawn from the public, and skilled photographic artists removed the dead person to create a new official version. Stalin's censors literally altered history by doctoring primary sources.

WHO'S WHO?

GEORGE ORWELL

This British author wrote two of the most famous books in the world. *Animal Farm* is an allegory of the foundation of the Soviet Union, with Stalin portrayed as a pig named Napoleon. Perhaps more famous is *1984*, which tells of a future country ruled by Big Brother. Everyone is constantly watched by Big Brother and a Ministry of Truth censors old documents to create a fake version of history.

HERE'S SOME GOOD NEWS

One way to censor bad news is to fill newspapers with good news instead. Countries with a lot of bad news to hide—for example, North Korea—have a single official news agency which only puts out positive stories about the country and its leader. As well as embellished stories about military might and economic success, North Korea's journalists write about the astounding feats of their leaders. One fake claim is that Kim Jong-un, the current leader, learned to drive at the age of three!

FOLLOW THE CROWD

In 1951, the American **psychologist** Solomon Asch experimented with the power of peer pressure. A test subject joined a group of people who were secretly working for Asch. The group was asked simple questions with an obvious answer. One by one the group members gave the wrong answer. Most test subjects followed the crowd with the wrong answer. This human behavior helps to entrench propaganda. Few of us want to stand out among our peers and call out fakery, especially if the divide between truth and falsehood is unclear.

Psychologists have discovered a phenomenon called the "illusory truth effect." When assessing if something is true or false, a person compares it with what they already know, and they are drawn unconsciously to what seems familiar. When false information is repeated often enough, people begin to think it is true, and base what else is true on this false information.

MANUFACTURING CONSENT

In a democracy, people are ruled by consent. A leader is given authority over everyone else because they won the most votes. People vote based on what they hear about each **candidate** and that information is supplied primarily by journalists (that is, until recent years, but more on that later). We also know that news outlets adopt a political allegiance as a way of securing a healthy audience. Can you see where I'm going? Politicians and journalists use each other to achieve success. What does that do to the news we read?

WHAT'S WHAT?

NUDGE UNIT

No government of an advanced society is complete without a "nudge unit," which uses psychology to change public behavior. Governments usually attempt to do this by passing laws, but that isn't very effective for certain goals, such as boosting public health or reducing environmental damage. Nudge units find small changes that are easily adopted by people, for example, putting fruit near the checkout at supermarkets means people buy more fruit. Simple but effective.

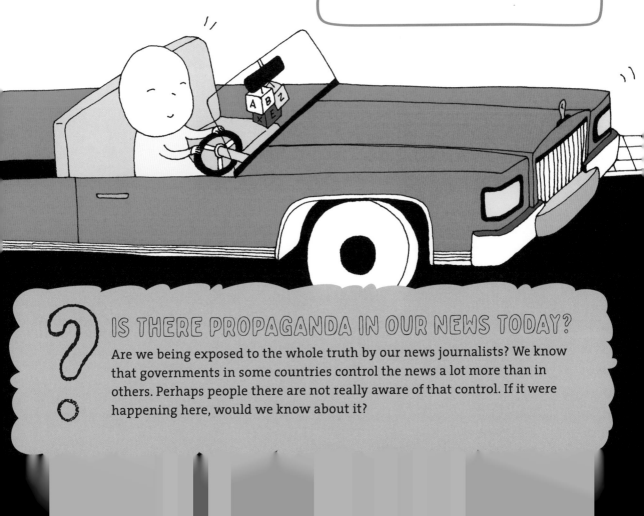

IS THERE PROPAGANDA IN OUR NEWS TODAY?

Are we being exposed to the whole truth by our news journalists? We know that governments in some countries control the news a lot more than in others. Perhaps people there are not really aware of that control. If it were happening here, would we know about it?

ADVERTISING

We are surrounded by messages that are deliberately one-sided. They are advertisements. Ads are not allowed to spread untruths but they are designed to catch the eye and promote a point of view in a way that stays with us. Mostly they use humor or strong emotions to get their message across in both text and images. The advertising industry developed to sell us products, but has lately been used to sell political ideas. We treat those messages differently than news—if we can tell the difference.

BRAND LOYALTY

There are three main purposes of advertising. The first is to introduce a completely new product. The ad needs to explain what the product does, how it is better than rivals, and also make you remember its name. Most ads you see are for products you already know. They say things you already know, over and over again. The purpose here is to build **brand** loyalty, and that comes into play when you are actually about to buy something. Have you tried out each product on offer? Probably not; so, given the choice, you go for the brand you know. The third kind of advertising appears in and around shopping areas, and its purpose is to clinch an actual sale for a product.

CHEAPER NEWS

Companies pay to advertise in newspapers. The same goes for TV ads, billboards, and web banners— see page 62. Advertising as we know it developed in the UK in the nineteenth century (although it's been around much longer than that). Back then, a newspaper's front page was full of text-only ads called "classifieds," placed by private citizens or small companies and paid for by the word. The income from ads pays for journalists to work and makes a profit for the owners. This makes the newspaper cheaper, or even free for the reader.

Advertising is so powerful that most countries place heavy controls on political ads. In general, ads are only allowed during election periods and they must focus on proposed plans for office, perhaps comparing them with opponents' ideas. The amount of money politicians can spend on ads is capped, which prevents richer politicians from having an advantage. Breaking these rules means the election may have to be run again.

WHAT'S WHAT?

SUPER PACS

In the United States, political advertising is largely unregulated. Politicians themselves are only allowed to make simple ads about why people should vote for them. However, a group of supporters, called a "Super PAC" (Political Action Committee), is allowed to raise money for an unlimited number of ads on behalf of a candidate. The politician has no official link with the Super PAC, so the ads are not constrained by the normal rules.

FAMILIARITY

In the 1960s, the psychology of advertising became clearer, when American researcher Robert Zajonc proved that we are drawn subconsciously to familiar things and are suspicious of the unfamiliar. This makes sense in the context of ancient society where anything out of the ordinary was potentially a deadly threat. Advertising short-circuits the system. If we are exposed to a set of branded messages long enough, we instinctively trust them.

IS ADVERTISING A WASTE OF TIME?

The money from advertising reduces the cost of many things, especially news and TV shows, which would otherwise fall on the consumer—people like you and me. Is it worth it? Imagine a world without ads. How would we find out about the stuff we need to buy?

GETTING PUBLICITY

An ad may entertain, annoy, or intrigue us but it can also contain useful information. We are rightly skeptical of what an advertising message tells us because it exists to sell us something. Whereas, news stories are simply worth paying attention to because they are supposedly true. So what if advertising a brand can be done through a piece of news? This is the job of publicists. Their job is to come up with ways of making a brand the feature of a news story.

You may have heard people say that there is no such thing as bad publicity. People who work in the public relations (**PR**) business seldom agree. Part of their job is to manage the reputation of a brand—in other words, keep bad news out of the public eye. To do that, they offer the journalist several different stories—some that promote the brand in question and others that might damage rival companies.

STUNTS AND PUFF PIECES

How do you get your new brand of tomato sauce, Krazy Ketchup, into the news? You could do it with a stunt. How about a team of skydivers dressed as tomato sauce bottles parachuting into a pool of Krazy Ketchup? That sounds dangerous—and expensive. The other option is a puff piece. Invite some journalists to tour the new factory as part of a luxury weekend break. In return, they may write a supportive story about the brand.

SPONSORSHIP

One of the most effective ways of getting a brand into the news is by sponsorship. A company pays for its name to be made part of an event or location likely to get into the news: the Krazy Ketchup Arena or the Krazy Ketchup Tiddlywinks World Cup. Even better, sponsor a sports team. Whenever that team wins, your branding will appear in the news.

EMBEDDED JOURNALISM

Armies have public relations experts too. If the wrong story leaks out during a war, it could affect things on the battlefield. Reporters go to war zones to keep the public informed of the events. No army wants to kill or injure reporters working on the front line, so they are placed with a combat unit, a practice called "embedding." Embedded journalists stay relatively safe as they witness the fighting, and additionally the army news officers control what they see, and what they don't see.

Stand by for a new word: "advertorial." It's an ad made to look like an editorial article. In most countries, there has to be a clear title saying that what you are looking at is not real news but a paid-for ad dressed up to look like it. A quick read is often enough to spell that out. Advertorials might look like news but they are written to sell products.

WHAT'S WHAT?

LOBBYING

There is a whole different side to public relations that happens in government buildings. In the past, this was done by literally waiting for politicians in the lobby outside Congress and grabbing their attention as they came and went. Today "lobbyists" work differently, but the job remains the same—to influence the decisions of lawmakers on behalf of their clients, who are often wealthy companies.

CAN YOU TELL THE DIFFERENCE BETWEEN NEWS AND PUBLICITY?

Whose job is it to figure out if a newspaper article, video, or other piece of information is actual news or a publicity stunt? Should it be the people who wrote it, or is it up to us to check the purpose of the story?

RADIO AND TELEVISION

Increasingly we do not read printed newspapers. Instead we get news from websites and apps or from the TV and radio. It's the same news so why does it matter? Well, it matters a lot. To begin to understand how, we'll need to rewind a bit and look at how radio and television services grew up over the last century.

Not long after speech radio was developed, television was invented. Many people had a hand in this, but the first workable system was created by John Logie Baird, a Scottish engineer, in 1926. Cinema movies were already a big thing by this time, but television captures and displays images in a different way—a way that can be transmitted using radio waves.

THE RISE OF RADIO

In the early 1900s, the Italian Guglielmo Marconi perfected a way of sending Morse code signals as pulses of radio waves. The waves were picked up by a receiver, which converted the code into a buzzing noise. Alongside this development, microphone and loudspeaker technologies were being developed for use in telephones and early sound systems. By the 1920s, the two were merged, so instead of codes, radios could send and play back any sounds, including the human voice.

BROADCASTING

Radio was developed as a two-way communications system. Television works in a similar way, connecting one camera to a single screen on a closed circuit (CC). The two technologies presented a new opportunity called "broadcasting." Weirdly, that term comes from farming. It means to throw seeds in all directions, hoping that some will land somewhere they can grow. The modern meaning of broadcast is similar: radio and TV signals are transmitted in all directions. The broadcaster can't control who receives the signals, but hopes someone will.

44

NEWSREELS

People first saw moving pictures of the news in the cinema. Before a film was played at the cinema, a short newsreel screened. Some cinemas showed only newsreels, mostly 30-minute reports that were updated every month. Stories with exciting visual scenes were selected over ones without. If a story wasn't caught on camera, fewer people got to hear about it. Politicians and other public figures quickly saw the need to be filmed regularly so they could be included in newsreels.

WHO'S WHO?

EADWEARD MUYBRIDGE

In 1872, Muybridge was asked to settle a bet: do horses lift all four feet off the ground when they gallop? Muybridge set up a dozen cameras along a racetrack and took a picture with each as the horse ran past. It took him 12 years to get it right! But his pictures proved that all four hooves leave the ground as the horse gallops. More to the point, projecting the photos in order created a moving picture of the horse. He'd made the first movie!

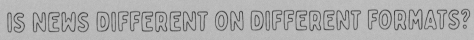

IS NEWS DIFFERENT ON DIFFERENT FORMATS?

Here's an idea. Pick a day and check the news online, on the radio, on TV, and in the newspaper. How do they compare? Are any stories covered by all the sources? Which ones? Can you figure out why some sources cover certain stories and others don't?

BROADCAST NEWS

Television and radio broadcasts are not all about the news. But the main channels provide news summaries throughout the day. News broadcasters have always had an advantage over printed news. They can report stories very quickly. Families began to organize their time around news **bulletins** as broadcasts brought up-to-the-minute reports right into the home.

NEWS BULLETINS

A newsreader lists the headlines in order of importance to get the attention of the audience. Then there is a report about each story generally using primary audio or video sources, including interviews with those involved. A reporter will explain the details. On TV news, animated visual aids help get the point across. Experts are asked to comment, and the opinions of ordinary people on the street may broadcast as "vox pops" (short for *vox populi*, which is Latin for "voice of the people").

NEWS ANCHOR

The main TV news bulletins are broadcast in the evening once young children are in bed. This means journalists can tell stories without censoring out alarming details. The host of the news program is called the "anchor." Anchors have to read the news in the same calm way, no matter what is going on, good or bad. Viewers will have a favorite anchor and tune in to watch their bulletins rather than those of a rival channel. The role of the anchor is even more important on rolling news channels, more of which on page 53.

FUNDING BROADCASTS

Most broadcast news is funded by advertisements. Channels sell advertising space, and ads appear before and after the news. There are government-set rules about how many minutes of ads are allowed each hour. It varies but it's about 15 minutes of ads for every hour of broadcast. Most countries also have a public service broadcaster paid for by taxation. The way these public broadcasters are linked to the government is crucial to how they report the news. Are they allowed to criticize the government who funds them? That's a complex subject which we'll look at more closely on page 74.

INTERNATIONAL BROADCASTS

Wealthy nations have international broadcasting services, such as the *BBC World Service*, *Voice of America*, and *China Radio International*. These organizations deliver news to foreign listeners mostly by radio broadcasts, in a wide range of languages. In most cases, international services are run by governments. Their purpose is to offer a view of world events that isn't available in other countries. The news output from foreign services always sounds different from the news you hear from your own country, and it's hard not to assume that it is propaganda. Nevertheless, a few international services have a global reputation for fair and **unbiased** reporting.

DO YOU PREFER TV NEWS OR A NEWSPAPER?

A TV news program is able to offer you a first-hand view of events and accounts from the people involved. However, there's limited time so only a few stories are covered. Do you think newspapers inform you better about what's going on?

TABLOID JOURNALISM

One way that the press can compete with broadcasters is through tabloid newspapers. The more respected newspapers are called "broadsheets" because they long retained the tradition of printing their news in dense type on large pieces of paper. A "tabloid" is a smaller newspaper with huge headlines on the front page and shorter stories inside. Tabloids are written in language that's much easier to read than a broadsheet. Nowadays, most broadsheet newspapers have adopted the tabloid format for cost reasons. People still have mixed views about traditional tabloids though. Some say they are a lot of fun; others regard them as a major source of division in society.

SCANDAL AND CELEBRITY

Tabloid newspapers are not all the same. They target a wide range of markets, such as commuters traveling on crowded buses and trains, young parents, retired people, or young people looking for a laugh. However, all tabloids devote a lot of space to the same subjects: gossip, celebrity, and scandal.

KEEPING IT SIMPLE

A tabloid journalist has to condense serious news stories into a short, simplified form. It is easy for some people to be scornful of this kind of "easy" news and dismiss the content of the story because of it. However, tabloid journalists are very skilled writers. Articles, especially those about politics, are written from a point of view that editors believe most reflects what readers already think. That saves having to explain both sides of a political argument.

The word "tabloid" was originally coined to refer to small tablets of medicine, compressed to make them easier to swallow. The first examples of tabloid journalism date from the turn of the twentieth century, and at first referred to the short, easily consumable news stories themselves. The smaller page size now associated with the term tabloid appeared in the 1920s.

WHO'S WHO?

JOSEPH PULITZER

You may have heard this name from the Pulitzer Prize, the top award in American journalism. The prize was funded by Joseph Pulitzer, one of the biggest publishers of tabloid news in the nineteenth century. In life, Pultizer's name was less prestigious than the prize. His reporters practiced "yellow journalism"—something like the tabloid stories of today—where readers were given sensational and often faked stories.

DELIBERATELY FAKED

Fake news has been a part of tabloid journalism from the start. In 1835, the *New York Sun* published a series of stories about how life had been discovered on the Moon, including a beaver that walked on two legs and a bear with a unicorn horn. The stories boosted sales. A few weeks later, the New York paper admitted it made it up—and no one really minded. Faking news can have more serious consequences, though. In the 1890s, tabloid owner William Randolph Hearst published false stories about how brutal Spain's rule over their colonies was. This turned Americans against Spain, and by 1898 the two countries were at war!

In 1903, the editor of the *Clarksburg Daily Telegram* was fed up with rival newspapers stealing his stories, so he set a trap. He printed news about how a Mr. Swenekafew had been shot over an argument about a dog. *The Daily News* printed the same story the following day. *The Daily Telegram* responded by showing that the Swenekafew story was made up—just read the victim's name backward!

TABLOID TRICKS OF THE TRADE

An ideal tabloid story is one that exposes the squalid secrets of celebrities, like musicians, sports stars, actors, and politicians. To find them, tabloid journalists "dig the dirt." Here are five ways they do it:

Snooping: Journalists literally get their hands dirty by sorting through the garbage thrown out by a celebrity to find clues about love affairs, a crime, financial problems, or whatever makes good "copy" (that's what journalists call a story).

Blagging: This is tricking banks, doctors, or companies into giving away secret information about a celeb.

Sting: A famous person is invited to a fake meeting and tricked into agreeing to do something that makes them look silly or bad—all caught on camera.

Hack: In the 1990s and 2000s journalists (especially in the UK) hacked into the private phone messages of thousands of people. This is against the law and several of the hackers went to jail!

Doorstepping: Once a story "breaks" (or becomes public), reporters from every other paper will wait outside the celebrity's house day and night, ready to get the latest picture and latest comment should the person appear.

Warning: These things can all be highly antisocial and can be illegal!

PAPARAZZI

This Italian word refers to photographers who follow celebrities around taking pictures of them. To avoid the "paps" celebrities might go out less, but then photographers simply try to snap pictures of them in private. Tabloid newspapers and gossip magazines buy the pictures. The price depends on how famous the celebrity is and what they're doing. A picture of a famous movie star doing something very ordinary, like buying a coffee, will be seen around the world. Less famous people would have to be seen doing something much more interesting to make the cut!

KISS AND TELL

'Checkbook' journalism is a tabloid practice where the paper pays for information. The payment might be for a picture taken by a member of the public, of a celebrity doing the wrong thing in the wrong place. It is also often for a "kiss and tell" story, where an old girlfriend or boyfriend tells all about their time with a celebrity.

Most famous people loathe being chased by paparazzi, but some aspiring superstars hate being ignored by the press. They want their picture in the gossip pages alongside established stars. So they fake pap shots. They arrange for photographers to meet them at the beach or walking in a cool part of the city. The pictures are taken from a distance, so they look like the photographer has just seen the minor celebrity by chance.

WHO'S WHO?

THE FAKE SHEIKH

This British tabloid journalist's real name is Mazhar Mahmood. He specialized in dressing up as a wealthy Arab prince and inviting celebrities to meetings offering them money to do outlandish acts or say indiscreet things. All the "stings" were recorded. The Fake Sheikh also got criminals to give away their plans—and the police then came to arrest them. However, in 2016, Mahmood was shown to have faked news and was found guilty of lying to police to get people in trouble, as well as make his stories better.

SHOULD TABLOID NEWSPAPERS BE ALLOWED?

Are tabloid newspapers harmless fun? Are they valuable for exposing wrongdoing and campaigning for justice? Or do they stir up trouble by bending the truth? How do we ensure they keep the right balance?

ROLLING NEWS

In the 1980s, a new kind of broadcast news service appeared—the "rolling news" channel. The first was the Cable News Network, CNN, an American channel that broadcast news bulletins 24 hours a day. CNN caused quite a stir. Few people watched it all the time, but during a major event, such as a war, terrorist attack, or natural disaster, CNN and similar all-news channels showed live pictures of what was unfolding. The news became the most exciting show on TV.

CNN and other news channels are available in all countries and have become a valuable source of news. However, that means news flows from "the West to the rest"—from rich countries to poorer places. Foreign viewers are frequently dissatisfied by reports, which appear biased or ignorant of local facts. As a result, local rolling news channels have been set up across the world.

SPEED OF NEWS

Two technologies made rolling news possible: cable television and satellite communication. The first made the news channel "subscription only" – you had to pay to watch because this kind of news is expensive to produce. The second allowed news crews to send video reports from anywhere in the world. The result was news got a lot faster, and that began to change the way viewers related to world events. One of these was the "CNN effect," where the public opinion was profoundly influenced by what they saw on the news.

TALKING HEADS

Most days are slow news days. There are plenty of stories to tell but most are complex and won't capture the interest of the majority of viewers. While they wait for the next big story, many 24-hour news channels fill the time by talking about the last big story. They assemble a screenful of "pundits," who have some expertise in the subject in question. More importantly they are able to talk clearly about the subject on live TV (quite a skill). Pundits represent a range of views and often argue with each other.

NEWS AND ENTERTAINMENT

Before rolling news appeared, nightly TV news bulletins aimed to transmit news in a fair and unremarkable way. However, as news channels began to compete for viewers, news had to be made more entertaining. Producers covered a wide range of stories and procured the most exciting video from around the world. As newspapers had done before them, TV news started targeting coverage at certain sections of the public, often by their political leanings. News anchors were allowed to give their opinions and argue with pundits who disagreed. The result was news that appealed to some viewers but looked fake to others.

WHAT'S WHAT?

THE NEWS CYCLE

Rolling TV news created a rhythm to the news. Few people were watching the news at night (unless something big was happening) but they switched on at breakfast to catch up on the big headlines of the day. The next time they tuned back in—at lunch time or in the evening—they wanted to see a different set of stories (or they'd switch to a rival channel)! And so a news cycle was formed, where stories only last for a few hours before being replaced by newer ones.

SHOULD WE LISTEN TO PUNDITS?

Discussions about the news between experts and interested parties on news channels is called "punditry." It can be entertaining and informative. However, pundits are not journalists and are often one-sided in their views. How could it be damaging to broadcast their opinions?

While tabloid journalism and rolling news is focused on reducing stories to a form that's quick and easy to understand, some journalists take a very different approach. They spend months, even years, investigating a complex subject, which is then set out in a series of long articles or a book. The subject of these investigations is often political corruption or crimes committed by companies. The stories not only expose these deeds, but also detail "cover-ups" where people have lied and hidden evidence to keep the truth secret. This is not really about fake news. Instead it is news about fakes and frauds.

WATERGATE

The most famous piece of investigative journalism concerned US president Richard Nixon—also known as "Tricky Dicky." Nixon had a personal team of "plumbers" who did not mend pipes but spied on political rivals by bugging offices and copying documents—all illegal. This became public after a break-in at an office at the Watergate building in Washington, D.C., in 1972. Journalists Bob Woodward and Carl Bernstein investigated, and piece by piece revealed Nixon's crimes. Two years later, the evidence against Nixon was so damning that he was forced to resign, the only US president ever to do so.

NELLIE BLY

Elizabeth Seaman was a pioneering investigative journalist in the late nineteenth century. She wrote under the pen name Nellie Bly. In her early career, she wrote about subjects that her editors thought interested women readers, but these topics didn't interest Nellie. In 1887 she agreed to pretend to be mentally ill so she could go to New York's notorious "lunatic asylum." Nellie reported back about her bad treatment during her ten days in the hospital, which forced New York to improve the care of the mentally ill.

START INVESTIGATING

Being an investigative journalist is a bit like being a private detective or police officer. The evidence is out there and it's your job to find it. Here are some of the ways to do that:

Company information: Every company has to be registered with the tax authorities, so it's possible to find out who owns the company, where it is based, and what it does with its money.

Public documents: A large amount of information is available to the public. This includes the results of court cases, applications for constructing new buildings, and government reports.

Freedom of Information (FoI): Most of what a government does is public, so journalists (or anyone) can put in a FoI request to find out what officials are doing.

The big question is where do you start looking for news?

An undercover documentary is a piece of non-fiction TV or film that covers true-life events. A journalist goes undercover with hidden cameras and recording equipment to investigate a subject from the inside. The reporter might join a gang, work in a prison, shop, or school, and collect evidence of wrongdoing. The recordings are edited together to show the public exactly what is going on. There's nothing fake about that.

WHISTLEBLOWERS

To "blow the whistle" means to publicize the illegal or immoral behavior of an organization or an important person. In the past, whistleblowers have exposed wrongdoing by banks, lawyers, soldiers, spies, and, of course, elected politicians. A whistleblower generally has to break some rules to make the facts public. They may face losing their job or even being sent to prison. A journalist can protect the whistleblower's identity, so the facts become public but the informant stays in the shadows. However, if the whistleblower is breaking the law, then a journalist is obligated to reveal their identity. They are faced with the choice to protect their source or go to prison themselves.

Some argue that investigative journalism is in decline. This is partly because it is very expensive to do, and partly because it does not make simple and engaging copy for tabloid and rolling news. News organizations that sell advertising are also accused of a conflict of interest. They need big companies to buy ads from them and are unlikely to do investigations into those companies—or do anything that might scare off other advertisers.

WIKILEAKS

One way a journalist can protect a whistleblower is to not know who they are. However, the whistleblower needs to provide very strong evidence of their claims. Whether they do that in person, by post or email, that secretive communication—known as a "leak"—can reveal their identity. The Wikileaks organization, among others, has created a system of anonymous communication that allows whistleblowers to pass on information without revealing who and where they are. This new way of leaking has resulted in vast amounts of information being made public, such as secret US government messages and the illegal financial activity of businesspeople.

PUBLIC INTEREST

Most news stories, at least the interesting ones, have winners and losers. An editor decides if the damage caused by a story outweighs its benefit to society as a whole. They ask themselves, "Is it in the public interest?" This is especially difficult to answer when it comes to leaked secrets because it is unclear who benefits and who does not from their publication. For example, publishing government secrets can put spies working undercover at risk.

Anonymous leaks are not always a good thing. What do you do if the material in the leak has been obtained illegally? During the 2016 US presidential election, the emails sent by the leaders of the Democratic Party, who wanted Hillary Clinton to be president, were stolen by hackers and made public by Wikileaks a few weeks before the vote. Journalists searched through the emails—most were boring—and reported on what they read. These stories turned some voters against Clinton, and her rival Donald Trump won the election. Something similar happened in the 2017 French election, but the law blocked journalists from reporting them so close to the actual vote. After the election, it was found that the hackers had added fake emails to make it look like French politicians were committing crimes.

WHAT IS THE PUBLIC INTERESTED IN?

The contents of the daily papers suggest that the public is more interested in stories about celebrities and sports than serious events in the world. Should editors supply stories that interest the public or stories that the public ought to know?

WHAT IS INFORMATION FOR?

The "new" in news refers to new information. Humans first spread information through speech and song, then painting and writing, and eventually printing and broadcasting. The communications revolution (we're in that right now) means all these types of communication have converged into one form: digital code. A computer records, replays, displays, and shares speech in the same way it does a painting or video—as a string of numbers or digits. And the way we use information has changed too.

THE HUMAN PROJECT

We humans think of ourselves as rational beings, because we use logic and reason to figure out what is true. However, we only started thinking like this around 350 years ago. People gathered new information to try to understand the universe. They thought using information in this way would improve our species, making us more rational and better. But we have a lot more information available to us now, too much for one human to understand, and that creates new opportunities.

POSTMODERNISM

By the 1980s, big thinkers had moved on into a "**postmodern**" mindset, questioning the idea that reason would lead to a true answer. So the rest of us started to distrust ideas based on logic alone. We prefer to make decisions using emotion as well. This change also means we no longer gather information for the purpose of progressing the human project. Instead it has become data to be bought and sold or analyzed to reveal new ways of making money.

The time when humans began using reason, logic, and science to separate fact from fiction is called the "Enlightenment." The Enlightenment was driven partly by the invention of printing, which allowed ideas to be recorded, copied, and shared. Many of history's greatest thinkers were Enlightenment figures. They include Isaac Newton, who defined gravity, Rene Descartes, the Frenchman who worked out existence, and Gottfried Leibniz, who wrote the first digital codes.

WHAT'S WHAT?

BIG DATA

There's so much information now that we can't make sense of it on a human scale. Small chunks of data collected for a certain reason are useful for revealing something interesting, but does all the data together tell us something? The answer comes from computer analysis, or "big data," which searches for patterns that we could never see.

FUTURE SHOCK

Imagine you're a newborn baby, just three hours old. You've just had some milk, and you want more, but you have to wait an hour. So you wait for a third of your life for your next meal! Imagine now that you are 90 years old. Waiting an hour is easy. This effect of time contraction is at work with information. Every hour, we collect more data than the hour before it. More information has been gathered about you, me, the world, and the universe in the last ten years than the previous 10,000 years.

EXPERTS OR EMOTIONS?

The world's a complex place, and we can't know it all. Who should we trust when it comes to getting information? Is it better to ask an expert human or the results of a big data analysis?

THE WORLD WIDE WEB

The news industry grew from the basic human desire to be informed. To begin with, the news was about the most significant and wide-reaching events, but gradually journalists and editors learned to target their news at a particular audience. Readers were largely passive consumers—they did not look for news, it came from newspapers and broadcast bulletins. That was it. But what if all the information you could imagine, and plenty you couldn't imagine, was available. You just needed to look for it. Well we have this system; it's the web. What has that done to the news?

THE INTERNET

The internet and the web are not the same thing. The internet is a system that connects computers into a network. There is a set of rules that control how data moves along these connections. If one route doesn't work, the rules automatically find another route, continuing until all the information has arrived. This system was developed in the 1960s to protect communication networks from attack in warfare. The web developed another 30 years after that—it is a system that lets users access information on computers connected to the internet.

EFFICIENT SHARING

The web was designed for sharing information across the world. To see how successful it was, let's rewind to an offline world. There are ten folders each containing ten pieces of paper, each located in a different city. To see if any of it was useful to you, you would have to travel to each city and look at every page in every folder. Fast forward to today. The same information is stored on ten computers. The information is made public via an internet connection so you can search through it from any device.

The rise of the web and other communications technology has meant that the way we discover news falls into two categories: push and pull. A newspaper is a "push" communication—the sender (the news editor) has control over what information we receive. A "pull" communication is one where the receiver has control of the content.

TIM BERNERS-LEE

The World Wide Web was invented in 1989 by English computer scientist Tim Berners-Lee. His aim was to make it easier for scientists to share information across the world. He created the first web browser for people, and his office desktop computer became the first web server holding the first website.

PORTALS

In the early days, the web was designed to be free to use and you, the user, were in control. As well as browsing other people's websites, you were free to maintain your own for the world to access. As the technology matured and started supporting pictures, videos, and games, most users opted to be web consumers, not web creators. The race began to attract these consumers to big websites that offered all kinds of useful information, not least the news. These sites became known as "portals," or the start points for a journey into the web.

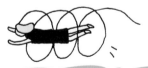

WHO HAS CONTROL?

The internet and the web have given control of information to ordinary people. When it comes to the news, is that a good thing? Should news always pass through an editorial filter to ensure it is clear, correct, and balanced? Or is it our job to check stories out?

WEB 2.0

By the start of the twenty-first century, the old web had changed into the **Web 2.0.** The technology had improved the front end, meaning how the web worked for us users. It was faster, you could stream live video and audio, and websites were delivering not only words and pictures but also animations and interactive elements. The technology had also made the back end more powerful—web companies could start making money from users. This was the start of the "attention economy," where users paid for services with their attention, measured in views. The challenge was how to keep people watching.

SEARCH

The first company to start creating Web 2.0 was Google. Google wasn't the first search engine though. Others, like Altavista and Lycos, competed to be the most popular web portal. Google was just so much better at finding what we wanted, and today more than 90 percent of searches start there—that's 63,000 requests every second! It has become so successful that these days we say "google" when we mean "search the web." Google is free to use. In return for its search, maps, translations, and email services, Google uses the information users give it to make money.

Web 1.0, the early web of the 1990s, did develop a key technology. Back then it was called "e-commerce" and today it is called "online shopping." E-commerce connected buyers and sellers and made it easy and safe to pay for things using the web. E-commerce also developed "suggestion engines," which made suggestions to buyers about other products they would be interested in. Such a system would find other uses on Web 2.0.

PLATFORMS

Web 1.0 was set up for users to create their own pages, but it required expertise to produce something even half decent. Web 2.0 fixed this problem: a company maintained the website and handled all the technical considerations, and the users created the content. The result was a new kind of media company: a platform. YouTube, Tumblr, and SoundCloud are all platforms which do not create their own content, the users do it. All that content encourages other people to visit the site. The clever thing is that the platform is making money from both creators and viewers.

WHAT'S WHAT?

PAY WALLS

Unlike other platforms, which are free to use, news platforms are often hidden behind a pay wall. You can only see a few hints and teases of the news and must pay a subscription to see the rest. After 20 years of getting everything for free, these pay walls seem quite expensive. Is news worth that much?

THE ALGORITHM

Once a web platform has your attention it works hard to keep it, using the suggestion engine. Today this system is normally referred to as the platform's algorithm. A platform's long-term success is closely linked to the algorithm. If we are not satisfied, we users will stream video and music somewhere else. The platforms are very good at giving us what we want based on our past activity. That's the easy part. The harder task is how the algorithm figures out how a song sounds, what a video is about, and what a news story says, so it can match that to our tastes. Do they always get it right?

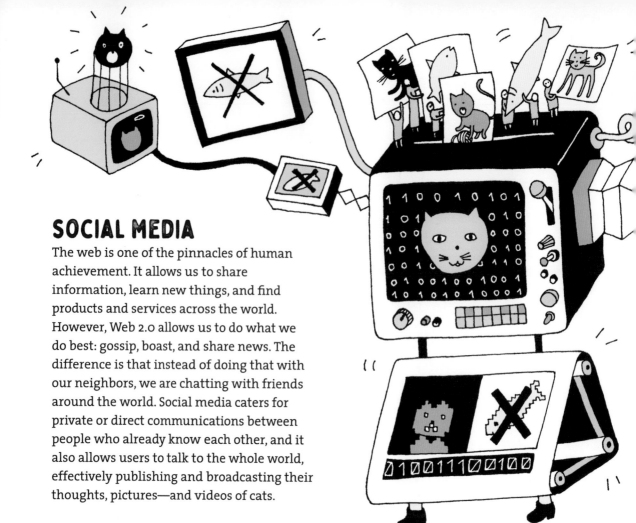

SOCIAL MEDIA

The web is one of the pinnacles of human achievement. It allows us to share information, learn new things, and find products and services across the world. However, Web 2.0 allows us to do what we do best: gossip, boast, and share news. The difference is that instead of doing that with our neighbors, we are chatting with friends around the world. Social media caters for private or direct communications between people who already know each other, and it also allows users to talk to the whole world, effectively publishing and broadcasting their thoughts, pictures—and videos of cats.

Algorithms are developed using a process called "machine learning." The software is tasked with identifying content—is this a video about cats? It learns to do this by trial and error, by comparing the digital code of videos, and trying to see a cat among the code. This system is surprisingly successful because it trains using millions of videos and eventually gets it right.

PSYCHOGRAPHICS

Every click, view, share, and like you make on social media is recorded and can be cross-referenced to your shopping habits, travel plans, and friends lists. In the same way that analysis finds patterns in your online profiles to suggest content and target ads, psychographic analysis claims to define your personality, your values, and your political opinions. That kind of information is very valuable. Psychographic analysis is pretty unreliable at the moment, but more data and better machine learning may soon change that.

WHAT'S WHAT?

THE SEMANTIC WEB

Also called Web 3.0, the semantic web would be able to understand the data it contains. We human consumers understand the web's content, but the algorithms used to search it, curate it, and present it to us do not. They are simply following rules set out by the web's protocols or those created by machine learning. A semantic web search engine would actively look for what you wanted and filter out what you didn't want, such as fake news.

The content of social media is created by you, the user. You create all the pictures, gifs, memes, and emojis. The platform then uses an algorithm similar to other platforms to figure out what ads to place into your feed. Each advertiser pays the platform to target people they know are already interested in their products. Does it work though? Do you see ads that appeal to you on social media? Have you ever clicked on one?

NEW AGGREGATORS

Social media platforms provide their users with a news feed. The platforms do not have reporters finding stories. Instead they gather or "aggregate" news from sources across the web. These stories may be curated by human editors, who pick out the top stories, but most are collected automatically. If you scroll through a newsfeed you might find that certain stories are repeated by different sources. Are they copying? Where did the story actually start?

WHO'S IN CHARGE OF THE WEB?

You pay for your social media feeds with your data and by watching ads. You knew that, of course, didn't you? What does the web exist for and is it limited by the way the platforms make their money? Is there another way of doing it?

MEMES

So where have we gotten to? Humans communicate using speech, writing, and pictures. We spread news to feel connected, and prefer stories and ideas that are easy to understand, especially if we can connect with them emotionally. So let's make a list of effective media: myths, books, paintings, photos, newspapers, and websites. And there is one more, something that can make use of any of the others. We call it a "meme."

THE MEME MEME

A meme can be a joke, a dance move, or a chain letter—any kind of idea that is easily spread among a group of people. Once these sorts of ideas were called "crazes," and the craze in one neighborhood would have been unknown to a visitor from another. Today the whole world can be aware of a meme, so much so that it becomes a global news story. And news—fake or real—can also be spread as a meme.

The world of memes is fast moving but here are some classics:

Rickrolling Entice someone to click on something interesting only to find it is really a video of Rick Astley singing a song from the 1980s.

Harlem Shake Making videos of people dancing to a track ("The Harlem Shake") according to particular rules. It's complicated to explain; search for yourself.

Ice Bucket Challenge A charity fund-raising meme where you video yourself pouring a bucket of ice water over your head, only before you do, you challenge others to do it.

Hello to Jason Isaacs Just say "Hello" to Jason Isaacs.

You've probably never heard of any of these—they're no sooner the latest thing than they're gone!

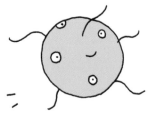

MEMETICS

The term "meme" comes from an idea called "memetics," which was invented in 1976 by English biologist Richard Dawkins. Dawkins is an expert in genetics, especially in the way genes mutate and evolve over time. He suggested that ideas evolve too—and that some were better at it than others. Like a gene, a meme only exists in order to be passed on and multiply in number. A gene does this by helping a lifeform survive and breed. A meme has an easier journey. It spreads and multiplies by appealing to people enough that they tell their friends about it.

GOING VIRAL

When the meme is being shared on social media it can spread incredibly fast in a phenomenon called "going viral." This is another biological comparison. A virus, like the ones that give us a cold, works by invading one cell and making millions of copies. All those copies then invade other cells, and the process repeats. In the same way, one share of a meme can lead to hundreds of people seeing it and sharing it. Now thousands of people can see it and they share it to thousands more. Within hours, millions of people will know the meme.

WHAT'S WHAT?

GUERRILLA MARKETING

Memes created a new avenue for advertising known as "**guerrilla** marketing." The word "guerrilla" originally referred to a small band of soldiers who appeared as if from nowhere, made a big attack, and then disappeared. Instead of buying advertising space, guerrilla marketers try to promote brands using memes. If they get it right, the public will distribute the brand message across the world for free!

ARE MEMES JUST HARMLESS FUN?

Of course the answer to this must be yes—unless of course the meme is hateful toward a section of society. However, what do memes do to the way we take in information? Do we ignore ideas if they are not a fun meme?

CONSPIRACY THEORIES

Now for the real truth! The publisher, editor, illustrator, and I are all working together—and none of you know anything about it. Not until you get to this chapter anyway, and by then it will be too late, we'll have finished the book! Sounds exciting when I say it like that doesn't it, like there has been some kind of conspiracy? A "conspiracy theory" proposes that what is presented to us as history or truth is in fact faked by powerful conspirators. The theories make really intriguing stories that tell of a hidden reality. Can you believe that?

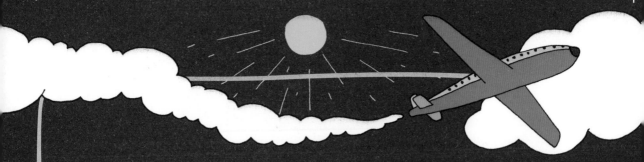

TRUE OR FALSE?

A "conspiracy" is a secret plan by bad people to do bad things. Conspiracies are real, just ask a police officer, but what do you make of these conspiracy theories:

Chemtrails: Have you ever wondered why high-flying jets leave a cloud-like trail behind them? The scientific answer is that they are caused when water vapor, blasting from the engines, is suddenly turned to tiny specks of ice as it meets the cold air. But could it be because the trails are filled with mind-control drugs?

Denver Airport: This airport serving the capital of the US state of Colorado covers a vast area, the second largest of any airport. Why so big? Is it because Colorado is a big state with a lot of empty land? Is it because it's located near the middle of North America and so is very busy with flights arriving from all over the world? Or is it because the airport is built on top of an underground city, which is the headquarters of a secret world government?

WHO'S WHO?

ILLUMINATI

It is often unclear who is running these conspiracies—I guess that's the point! Theorists point to a secret, all-powerful group, often called the "Illuminati." The Illuminati is, or at least was, real. It was set up in 1776 in Germany by a group of intellectuals who wanted reason and logic to dominate public life. The group was banned by the king and the Church, but people thought that these clever conspirators continued in secret and started to blame the Illuminati for all kinds of things—and still do!

Moon landings: NASA faked the Moon landings in a studio, firstly because it was much cheaper than actually going there, and secondly because the radiation in outer space is dangerous to humans. These are both good points, but the conspiracy theorists' proof mostly comes from things seen in Moon landing photos and videos that seem impossible on the Moon. It takes some explanation, but these are all easily dismissed. Plus, if the Moon landing was faked, all 400,000 people who worked on the Apollo Program would have kept the secret for the last 50 years. How likely is that?

Global warming: Is the climate changing? Is the world warming up because of the way humans burn fossil fuels? Climate scientists all say yes. However, the scientific evidence is falsified, say others (who are not scientists), and the reason is to...well, why would you make it up? Donald Trump, for example, has said China did it to make Americans poorer.

Flat Earth: Despite what experts have been saying since the days of Aristotle, 2,300 years ago, some say our planet is not a spherical globe but a flat disc. Flat earthers argue that if it were a globe, all the water would fall off and you would not be able to see anything in the distance. All the pictures taken from space are fakes.

HAVE THEY GOT A POINT?

Conspiracy theories are definitely strange, but they say truth is stranger than fiction, right? There are many examples of governments spreading misinformation and propaganda that is later shown to be false. And powerful people do conspire to cover up their wrongdoings, such as during the Watergate scandal. So could conspiracy theorists be on to something?

SEEING THE LIGHT

Do carrots help you see in the dark? In World War II, RAF bosses claimed their pilots ate carrots so they could see better. A lack of vitamin A will make you go night blind (you can still see in the day) and carrots are a good source of vitamin A. But the pilots hadn't really developed super-vision. This story was told to conceal the fact that the planes they were flying used secret radar tech to find the enemy.

COLD WAR SCARE STORIES

Communists who wanted Russia to rule the world were at work in secret across America from the 1930s to 1960s. They could be anyone anywhere!

SECRET MIND CONTROL

From 1953 to 1973, the CIA was running the top-secret Project MKUltra which investigated how drugs could be used to control people or make them tell the truth. Some test subjects went on to be famous authors and musicians (and a few became mass murderers)!

WHY DO PEOPLE BELIEVE CONSPIRACIES?

Go on admit it, there will have been a time when you heard a conspiracy theory and thought, "that sounds possible." What was it about—the Roswell Incident, 9/11, the Kennedy assassinations? A few people believe that history is all faked and that conspiracy is everywhere. Psychologists have theories about why people think like this:

- A conspiracy is a projection of a person's own bad feelings and deeds. They can't admit it about themselves, but see it in everyone else.
- People who believe in conspiracies tend to be okay with lying and cheating and assume that everyone else is as well.
- People who feel they have no power to change their lives are comforted by the idea that their problems are caused by a hidden force they can do nothing about.

WHO'S WHO?

SHOCK JOCKS

Conspiracy theories are often spread by "shock jocks," who are broadcasters that get attention, and a bigger audience, by being outrageous. Any big news event is then explained in terms of a particular conspiracy. Over the years, these figures and their audiences have created an entire world view based on conspiracy theories.

There are four kinds of conspiracy theory:

- A threat is coming from outside the community, perhaps from a foreign nation.
- The conspirators lurk among us and could be anyone. Even you...or me!
- A small group of super-rich and super-powerful people are secretly in control.
- A street-level conspiracy is preparing to take over.

SPREAD THE WORD

People love a good story. A conspiracy theory has two compelling story elements. It has its own clear internal logic, so it makes sense within itself like a well-written fantasy or sci fi tale. It also has a great twist—in the end you get to find out what is really going on. Conspiracy theorists need to spread these stories and like to meet up with fellow believers. An individual's belief in the theory is strengthened by the fact that they are part of a community.

ARE CONSPIRACY THEORIES GETTING MORE POPULAR?

The web is filled with all kinds of information and discussions about conspiracy theories. The sense is that this way of thinking is getting more common and spreading to more people. Is that true or just a conspiracy theory?

CITIZEN JOURNALISM

Before the web, a journalist could only operate if they had a job on a newspaper or as a broadcaster. A journalist was a useful person to know if you wanted to make something public. Now that power has been diminished because the web means anyone can share a story with the world. This kind of news-gathering is called "citizen journalism." It frees news from the control of big business and governments. Does that sound good? Let's investigate.

THE BLOGOSPHERE

The word "blog" is short for "web log" and originally meant a kind of online diary. Blogs became a big thing as Web 1.0 upgraded to 2.0. They could be about anything from a fun day out with the family to a piece of serious journalism. Hundreds of millions of blogs have been set up, and now they are linked through social media to create a "blogosphere"—a world of information created by independent writers or "bloggers."

THEORIES AND STORIES

Why blog when you can microblog instead? In 2006, Twitter was founded. It gave members 140 characters to write out their thoughts, ideas, anything they could think of r...Sorry, ran out of characters! It is not easy to say something meaningful in so few words, so Twitter upped the limit to 280 characters. In 2010, Instagram launched for people to communicate with pictures, soon followed by Snapchat. New forms of communication arose, the Twitter thread and Insta story, where the meaning is conveyed in a string of posts. Today, reporters break news stories as Twitter threads just minutes after learning the facts. News has never been so fast!

PODCAST

The term "podcast" is a mashup of "iPod" and "broadcast." A podcast can be a comedy, drama, discussion, or documentary. It is normally a piece of audio (although there are also video podcasts) of a kind that were once only available as a radio or TV broadcast. The difference is that while you might miss a broadcast, you can stream or download a podcast to listen anytime. And anyone with a microphone can make a podcast.

WIKIMEDIA

A guy I met said that Wikipedia, the online encyclopedia, was the most popular website in the world. However, that isn't true, it's the tenth most visited site. I got that information about Wikipedia from Wikipedia. It holds the largest collection of knowledge ever assembled so it's a really good place to look for information. However, as its name suggests, Wikipedia is a "wiki," which means the content can be altered by anyone. So has Wikipedia got it right or is the guy I met correct? You should be skeptical of what you read on Wikipedia (you can always check the references it provides), but you should also have a healthy skepticism of all information—especially if it's given away for free.

WHAT IS THE PURPOSE OF FREE NEWS?

Citizen journalism can look and feel the same as news released by established newspapers and broadcasters, but that does not always mean it has the same purpose. Why is it free? Is it promoting a particular viewpoint or brand? Is it really news or propaganda? Should you be asking the same questions about all news outlets?

FREEDOM OF SPEECH

You have the right to think whatever you want, because thinking is not the same as doing. You also have the right to say your thoughts out loud so others can hear them, but that right is balanced against other rights. You must limit noise in public space, so you don't disturb people in private spaces. And you cannot use your freedom of speech to call for violence or hate toward others. Simple? Well, no, that's just the easy parts. Let's look at less clear-cut issues of freedom of speech.

FREEDOM OF PRESS

The press does not have quite the same freedom of speech as you or I. Different rules apply in different countries, and these rules are frequently tested. A famous example was the *Pentagon Papers* scandal in 1971. These were documents that showed how the US government was spreading fake news about the success of the Vietnam War. The US government said printing these official secrets was illegal, but a judge decided that it was not, saying: "The security of the nation is not at the ramparts alone. Security also lies in the value of our free institutions. A cantankerous press, an obstinate press, a ubiquitous press must be suffered by those in authority to preserve the even greater values of freedom of expression and the right of the people to know."

THE RIGHT TO OFFEND

Social media means that our public speech is no longer limited to talking in the street to passersby; we can now speak to the whole world. What you say might not break any laws, but it might upset someone who reads it. Some of the rudeness may be deliberate or it may be due to ignorance or insensitivity about race, religion, or sexuality. Is being rude to one person, face to face, different than being rude to millions? Is the important thing the insult itself or the impact of that insult?

LIBEL AND SLANDER

Have you ever spread a rumor that you weren't sure was actually true? It's easy to do when it's a good story. However, spreading false rumors about someone is called "slander" and if you publish those falsehoods it becomes a "libel," which is generally taken more seriously. To slander and libel is to use lies to make someone look bad, and their right to protect their reputation trumps your right to say whatever you want. The difficulty arises when a journalist can't prove an allegation is true. The laws of libel can be used to prevent true events from being reported.

WHO'S WHO?

EDWARD SNOWDEN

In 2013, this American computer scientist who had been working for the secret intelligence services of the United States blew the whistle on how his country, working with several others, accessed people's phone calls, emails, and computer activity. That included world leaders, companies, and even you, if they wanted to. Snowden's complaint was that these spies were not fully under control of elected politicians and that was bad for everyone. He argued that even if the government allows freedom of speech now (including criticizing the government), they already have the power to stop us in the future. The Federal Government of the United States filed a lawsuit against Snowden, complaining his memoir, *Permanent Record*, violated non-disclosure agreements he had signed. They wanted to seize the profits Snowden would earn from the book.

ONLINE OFFENSE

If you are offended by something you have three choices: you can a) ignore it, b) be rude back, or c) explain why it is offensive. For online offense there is a fourth choice, to report the comment. Which is the right choice?

THE FILTER BUBBLE

Something strange is happening on the internet. Remember that digital communications were meant to make it ever easier for us to talk to each other? Well, the opposite is happening. The technology is so good at supplying us with access to what we want—our friends and the things we like—that we are blocked from hearing about people and things we don't like. The search and suggestion algorithms create a "filter bubble," which removes anything and anyone that challenges, offends, or bores us. Let's burst that bubble.

PERSONAL SERVICES

You only have yourself to blame. You didn't mean to do it, but you created your own personal filter bubble. The algorithms of web platforms are there to curate the content you see to keep you online for longer. By "content" we mean everything from ads, short-term "flash" offers when shopping, which friends' posts appear on your feeds, what video to watch next, and what news stories to read. Every click you make is used by the algorithm to create a personal profile which matches you with an ever-updated set of content. This way you only see materials that are similar and familiar to what came before.

ECHO CHAMBERS

Remember how conspiracy theorists like to stick together because it helps them feel like their ideas are normal? This is an idea called "communal reinforcement." Not only does it make us feel more secure in our beliefs, what we think gradually aligns with everyone around us, so we all end up thinking more or less the same thing. The filter bubble around your online existence creates a community of like-minded people, who all do and say similar things. This creates an echo chamber where you largely hear what you have already said yourself.

BELOW THE LINE

Often shortened to BTL, this is the thread of comments and replies that grows beneath an online news story, a blog, or a tweet. The commenters respond to the original article and some may start to discuss with each other. The threads can include heated debates and may include a lot of trolling, but they can also be quite dull! However, they do offer a glimpse of activity outside of your filter bubble.

The filter bubble can create a strong community bond, because everyone inside it offers support to each other. If one person offends another (whether on purpose or by accident), the community as a whole will rapidly take a side (usually turning on the offender). Other members might remove the offender from their feeds and messages and so they are blocked from the bubble. This is called "canceling" and can be a form of bullying.

TROLLING

One thing that stands out in a filter bubble is someone who disagrees with you. On occasion this can spark an interesting debate. But sometimes it's initiated by a troll who is deliberately seeking out online views that they disagree with, just to start an argument. However, trolling is in the eye of the beholder. You might regard a person who enters your social media bubble and politely challenges your way of thinking as an annoying troll—and block them. But who is actually behaving badly?

CHECK YOUR BUBBLE

Are you in a filter bubble? How do you tell? The answer is probably yes, but is it automatically a bad thing? A bubble filled with friends sounds quite nice. However, what can you do to make sure the bubble does not limit what you learn about the world?

MEDDLING AND MISINFORMATION

We've explored the nature of news and seen how it changes depending on how it is communicated and by whom. The truth of a story can get warped and certain stories are given great significance while others are largely ignored. None of this is a good thing, but we, the audience, can judge whether we are getting a balanced view of news. If not, we can look elsewhere for alternatives. But imagine news that is deliberately faked, sometimes very obviously, sometimes less so. Imagine this misinformation being used as a means of disrupting governments and meddling in elections. Are you confused by it all? Well, that is exactly what it is trying to do.

PARODY

What if it is all a big joke? Well, a lot of fake news is **parody**, which is a kind of copy that is designed to make a subject look silly. News parodies draw inspiration from real people and events but are a generally absurd—and very funny—version. A good parody will be almost identical to the truth, and part of the fun is spotting that it is a funny piece of fakery.

Some parody sites create fake news that isn't meant to be funny at all. Its purpose is to get attention and attract clicks. And everyone clicks—both those who think it's true and those who don't. These two groups then have BTL (below the line, remember?) arguments, and share the news/parody and associated controversy to friends. All this traffic generates revenue for the website.

STIRRING UP TROUBLE

Items of fake news are not just good for making money as clickbait (posts designed to encourage you to click on a link), they can be used to change the mood of the nation. The goal is to spread discontent, and just like online news parody, this fake news is designed to appeal to a particular target audience that does not trust the government or another section of the community. The result is a divided society with fake news that feeds people's prejudices and fears being shared within filter bubbles of like-minded people.

TROLL FARMS

Phew, exposing and explaining fake news is hard work. That is kind of the point. It isn't difficult to debunk a false story but it takes a lot of time and effort. By the time you've explained it to someone, it has spread to hundreds more, and new fake stories are always appearing. It also takes work to create the fake news, but there are people paid to do it in secret organizations called "troll farms." The troll farms create fake social media accounts, called "sock puppets." The sock puppets post and share fake news and stir up division BTL.

WHO'S WHO?

TWITTERATI

Are you a member of the Twitterati? This is a pun on the term "literati" which refers to people who love to read about and discuss literature. In the same way the Twitterati are avid users of Twitter. They may start a "pile on," where they take turns complaining about a tweet, which can wreck a reputation in minutes. Nevertheless, a pile on can also expose fake news and misinformation.

Government propagandists have tried to use misinformation to manage the mood of the nation for years, of course. However this isn't so easy today because most governments aren't in control of the news, especially not now it is spread online. So they've had to come up with other methods. One way of managing people's opinions of the nation is to confuse and deceive people by spreading fake news through social media.

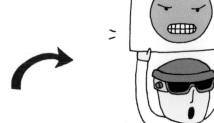

SOCBOTS

The more fake news there is, the more angry and confused we get. Human troll farmers are busy people, so social bots or "socbots" are used to automate some of the process. Socbots are artificial intelligences (AIs) that can post comments on social media. A human troll will direct a socbot toward a particular target on social media. The socbot will then post supportive messages using various identities. Despite being an example of AI, socbots aren't very smart and tend to repeat themselves. Nevertheless, in the mind of the public, they amplify a point of view, giving the impression that a lot of people believe a certain piece of fake news—when in fact no one does.

DEEP FAKE

Video has long been regarded as the best evidence you can get. If you catch the action on camera, no one can argue whether it happened or not. Sadly, technology has caught up with us, and now even video can be doctored. The deep fake system is especially good at changing a person's face. So far the technology is not really good enough to fool us every time. We humans are very good at spotting when something doesn't look quite right in a person's face. However, it will only get better. Perhaps it already has, and we haven't noticed...

Fake news became more complicated during the 2019 UK election. A Facebook group came up with a fun trick. They all posted the same word: "brilliant" under the news feed of a leading politician whom they liked. When his opponents said that he was being given fake support by bots, the Facebook tricksters revealed they were real. Next, the politician's opponents began to post things like "Brilliant"&name="Doris"syntax/ error" pretending that a socbot had gone wrong. They were faking fakers who faked fake news. It's true. Keep up.

ASTROTURFING

Astroturf looks like grass, it feels like grass, but it is not grass. In the same way "astroturfing" fills the web, especially comments sections, with fake views. The idea is that reviews represent the views of the grassroots, or the real people, and astroturfing creates artificial grassroots. Astroturfing is used as a kind of propaganda to make products and services seem more popular than they are.

USING DENIAL

The onslaught of news stories, some real, some fake, and some real stories about fake stories is never-ending. It's a full-time job keeping up with it all, and most people simply don't have the time. It's easier to just ignore all the news. But when something truly awful happens, a government can simply say, 'Oh, that's fake news.' Troll farms fill the web with conflicting information, and people don't give it much attention. Did it even happen?

WHO'S RESPONSIBLE FOR THE LIES?

Social media platforms say that they are not publishers or members of the press. That means they aren't responsible for the fake news that people share and view on their services. Do you think that's fair?

NEWS ABOUT NEWS

The scariest thing about fake news is how much we talk about it. (If you haven't noticed already, you're reading a book about it.) Fake news makes great real news. What was said, who said it, why they did it…Often the day's news includes a story about news or about how people are attempting to use the news to influence us. Pundits are asked to argue about things the rest of us can no longer remember happening. We do recall some things of course, but are they true?

A spin doctor's job is to defend their boss's reputation. When bad news appears about a product or a politician, the spin doctor prepares a rebuttal. Within minutes they have their side of the story ready and make sure every news editor includes it each time the story is repeated.

SPIN DOCTORS

Got a news problem and don't know who to call? Send for the spin doctor—an expert at putting over a certain point of view. They spin the facts to make them sound just right. Spin doctors are very persuasive people. They may represent the views of a brand or company but the top spinmeisters work for political parties. During elections political leaders hold TV debates, which cover many different topics. As soon as the debate ends, the action shifts to the "spin room" where spin doctors reorganize what you just heard into a simple message: "My person is better than the other person!"

PROCESSOLOGY

Spin doctors used to work best out of sight. However, today they have become part of the story. As a result, news, especially political journalism, often gets bogged down in the process of how things happened and who said what to whom, rather than what actually happened. This is called "processology," and it is of great interest to people who spend their lives gossiping about politics. However, to the rest of us, the processology is not the main issue—although we only ever hear what the issues are when political journalists report them…

SOUND BITES

If someone wants to get noticed they need to create a "sound bite." This is a short clear piece of audio or video that can be played in a news report or shared on social media. This is how to get the message across, and it means that journalists seldom have a chance to question the motives and the facts presented by the speaker. In the fast-moving world of news, the sound bites just go out without commentary or criticisms. Those might come later of course, but that is just another news story about a news story.

WHAT'S WHAT?

PUBLIC SERVICE BROADCASTER

State-run broadcasters are free from the influence of advertisers and thus they should be able to say whatever they want. That's the theory anyway. It all depends on who is in control of them. The oldest public broadcasting service is the BBC (British Broadcasting Corporation) which was set up by a Royal Charter in 1927 (although it began broadcasting in 1922). This legal declaration said that the BBC would be paid for by the government but granted the broadcaster total editorial independence. Other state broadcasters are simply publicizing what a government wants you to hear. How easy is it to tell the difference?

? DEFENSE FROM FAKE NEWS

Is the media our best defense against fake news? Or does the media create its own fake news? Or is it really all up to us to spot fact from fake?

83

POPULISM

The rise of fake news—or at least our increased interest and awareness of it—has come hand in hand with a rise in **populism** across the democratic world. Populists seek to gain political power by saying that they, and they alone, truly represent the people. Until they came along, other politicians, the civil service, and the media were all really working together to keep everything the same to suit themselves. A populist says he or she will change all that. Is populism something to watch out for or is it all fake news meant to scare us?

PEOPLE VS ELITES

The term "populism" doesn't relate to politicians saying whatever makes them popular. Instead it is focused on splitting a nation into two groups: the populus (the people) and the elites. The populists say the elites are fakers who lie about what is really going on and cover up their deeds. Populists urge us to be suspicious of everything our leaders say. That's fair enough, but who gains?

ENEMIES OF THE PEOPLE?

The elites are both the people in power and the people who benefit from that power. Just exactly where that divide falls is open to question, but everyone can agree that the people who make the laws, administer the country, and supply justice are the elites. These are elected politicians, civil servants, and judges. Together they form the basis of a functioning democracy, and they are all under attack by the populists.

Populists are often not linked to big political parties because the members of these parties are part of the elites that they oppose. With no party, populists don't have spin doctors to promote their message, so they need different ways of communicating with the people. Social media like Instagram and Twitter is a very direct route, but also a newspaper or TV news channel might choose to follow or support a populist politician. The politician gets exposure and in return the media gets a bigger audience.

A state that is truly run to benefit just a small elite is called an "oligarchy," a word that comes from the Greek term for "few rulers." Ironically, oligarchies generally have a populist leader as the chief public figure, with a secretive group around them that supports and controls their activities.

WHAT'S WHAT?

GREAT FIREWALL OF CHINA

Just as China was once protected by a Great Wall, the country's rulers now control what its people can view on the web using the "great firewall." A firewall is an online security measure which blocks unauthorized access. China's firewall blocks social media, search engines, and other information from outside China. The Chinese people still use social media and shop online, but using services hosted inside the country. The great firewall filters out news that might draw into question how China is ruled by a very small elite.

LEFT-RIGHT, LEFT-RIGHT

Left-wing politics focuses on the people as a group and tries to make everyone equal within it. Left-wing populism takes advantage of the idea of class conflict, where the divisions between the common people and the elites are due to in-built inequality based on the family you were born into. Right-wing politics focuses on the individual in the belief that a just society is one where people are in charge of themselves. In their beef with elites, right-wing populists draw on nationalistic ideas to get people's attention. These ideas propose that the country needs to protect itself from foreign influence.

THINK OF A POPULIST

I have deliberately avoided mentioning any politicians who use populism. Can you think of any yourself? Perhaps discuss your list of populists with friends. You might find they have a different opinion about who makes the cut.

HOW TO SPOT FAKE NEWS

We live in a world where everyone, from the leaders of the most powerful countries to eccentric conspiracy theorists, blames the world's ills on fake news. If you are feeling overwhelmed then I don't blame you. However, remember that the truth is a real thing. Here is a handy guide to help you tell fact from fake.

Always check the date, especially when a story is posted on social media. A clever trick used by trolls is to repost old stories from reputable sources. The story was true when it was written (probably years ago) and no longer relates to any public figures around today. However, the headline of the story does not make that clear. It could say, "City boss agrees to pave over popular park." However, the story is ten years old, and the city boss has changed since then. Unless you read the whole story, you may not realize that.

CHECK THE SOURCES

Don't just believe what you read. A story will link to an original source, perhaps an online newspaper or a blog. Take some time to find out more about the source. Read its other stories to find out about who runs the site. Check out the author, too. They will have a "byline" which often links to their other work. (If there is no writer credited, you can probably ignore the story.) You may find that the author and this website, paper, or platform is obviously interested in promoting a certain point of view using their news stories. There's nothing wrong with that, but it's the kind of thing you need to know.

CONFIRMATION BIAS

Make sure you are not letting yourself believe a story just because it seems to fit with what you already know (or think you know). This confirmation bias works the other way—if news is telling you something you do not like the sound of then you won't believe it. Recognizing that you might be biased in how you view news is all you need to do. You may be right all along, but just check to be sure. A good way to do that is to find the same story written by different media outlets. Each one will be biased in some way, so the truth is probably somewhere in the middle.

WHO'S WHO?

WILLIAM MUMLER

This nineteenth-century photographer became famous for taking portraits of people in which their dead relatives appeared as ghosts. Mumler was doubling up pictures of the subject with an earlier photo of their relative. His most famous fake was of President Abraham Lincoln (assassinated six years before) looming behind his wife Mary. She chose to believe that the photo was real. The moral here is don't believe stories just because they make you feel better.

TALK ABOUT IT

If you are still unsure about whether the news is real or not, you could talk to someone about it. Even if it is true, chatting through what it means might help you understand it better and figure out how you feel about it. Ask a teacher, parent, or better still a librarian to help you understand something. A librarian's job is to guide you through sources of information to find stuff out and understand it.

CAN WE SOLVE FAKE NEWS?

How do we fix the fake news problem? Perhaps we could issue licences for journalists which means only trained and approved people could report news. But would we be able to trust the people who approved the journalists? It might make the situation even worse! What do you suggest?

TRUE OR FALSE?

We've taken a long hard look at communication, journalism, and of course fake news. How do you feel about it now? Do you think we are on top of the problem and together we can sort out the mess? Or do you think this is a post-truth world where facts don't matter? Will whoever shouts the loudest and frightens, angers and excites people the most end up in charge? There is a lot to take in and weigh up. It might help to think about the different ways we can settle on what is true and what is false and how we seek to get our point across.

GET REAL

There are two kinds of reality: objective and subjective. Objective reality refers to the objects and events in the world around you that can be observed and verified by other people. If something is an objective fact, there can be no argument about it. It happened at a certain time at a particular place. Full stop. Objective reality sits within subjective reality. This is much bigger because it contains all of your thoughts and emotions as well as fantasies, dreams, ideas, and any other fictions created within your imagination. These are real to you only.

SUBJECTIVE TRUTH

Do you know what rhetoric is? That's a rhetorical question, so there is no need to answer. I only asked the question to illustrate the concept of rhetoric. Rhetoric is the art of persuading. It aims to win an argument using figures of speech and composing sentences in the most compelling way. Adding extra facts would be a help, sure, but sometimes there are no facts to use, and all that is left is rhetoric. So what am I driving at? (That's another rhetorical question.) Well, there is a lot of rhetoric out there. Politicians, spin doctors, and op-ed journalists use it all the time. The power of their statements comes from the way they use words, as well as the facts that underlie them. Admire the rhetoric, sure, but don't forget to focus on the facts.

OCCAM VS OSCAR

Occam's razor is a problem-solving system named after William of Ockham, an English monk from the thirteenth century. The idea is actually much older than this and it wasn't actually Ockham's idea—maybe that explains why his name is spelled wrong. Anyway it is more correctly called the "canon of parsimony," and simply put it says the simplest answer tends to be the right one. But when it comes to fake news does Occam's razor still cut it? It seems to me that it works the other way around. The truth behind fake news is always complicated, much more so than the faked news itself. Oscar Wilde, the Irish writer, said it this way: "The truth is rarely pure and never simple."

SYSTEM 1 OR 2

Psychologists have found that we make decisions in two ways. System 1 is ultra quick and is based on past experiences: "The last time something like this happened, I did this —and it worked! I'm doing it again." Back in the Stone Age, this kind of quick thinking, or intuition, could have been a lifesaver. However in the complexities of modern life, system 1 falls foul of our bias and ignorance: "The last time I read a story that said something like this, it was true. This must be true too." System 2 involves active thought where you weigh up the pros and cons. It takes a bit more effort, but unlike Stone Age people, you have the time.

OBJECTIVE
TRUTH

MIND MAP

The world of fake news is a confusing place. Even when news is entirely genuine, the facts are frequently blurred to support one point of view over another—usually the one that is the most appealing to the platform's viewers or readers. So it is hard to know where the real news ends and the deliberate lies, bluffs, and double bluffs begin. This mind map is here to show the many different types of communication that add up to make news media. It shows how they spread news but also how they can be used to spread lies. It will probably create more questions than answers, but the most important thing to do is to keep paying attention to the news. The more you know about current events all over the world, the better you will be at spotting the fakes. It's up to you now!

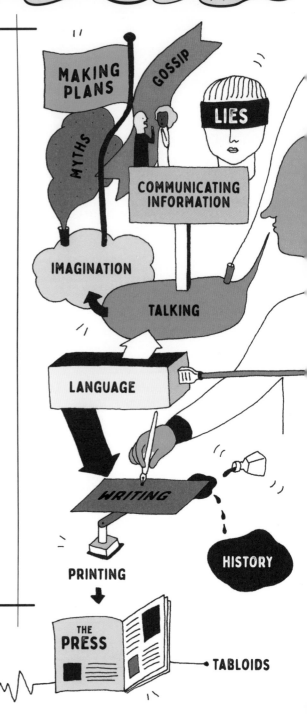

MAKING PLANS

GOSSIP

MYTHS

LIES

COMMUNICATING INFORMATION

IMAGINATION

TALKING

LANGUAGE

WRITING

HISTORY

PRINTING

THE PRESS

TABLOIDS

MEDIA BIAS

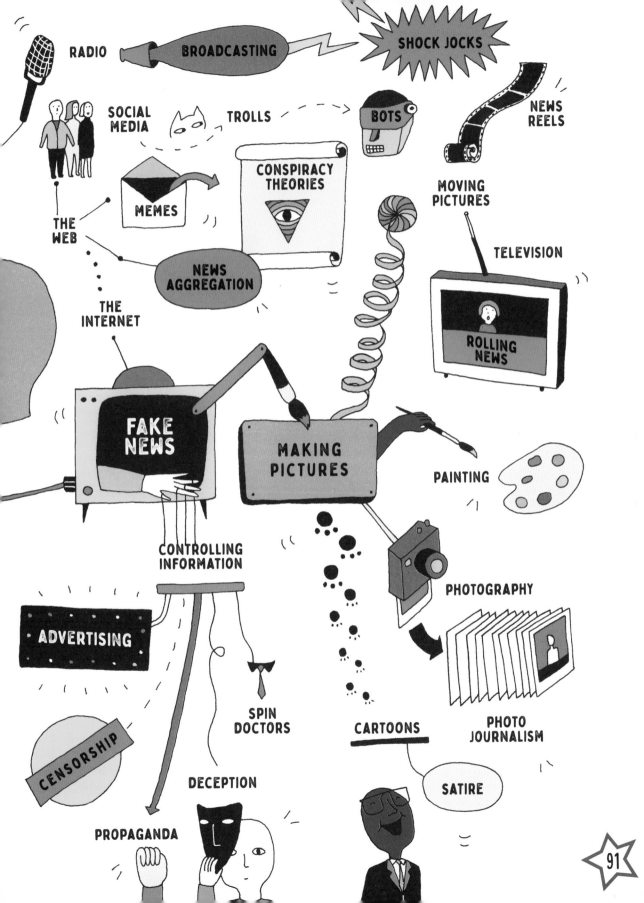

RADIO

BROADCASTING

SHOCK JOCKS

SOCIAL MEDIA

TROLLS

BOTS

NEWS REELS

MEMES

CONSPIRACY THEORIES

MOVING PICTURES

THE WEB

NEWS AGGREGATION

TELEVISION

THE INTERNET

ROLLING NEWS

FAKE NEWS

MAKING PICTURES

PAINTING

CONTROLLING INFORMATION

PHOTOGRAPHY

ADVERTISING

SPIN DOCTORS

CARTOONS

PHOTO JOURNALISM

CENSORSHIP

DECEPTION

SATIRE

PROPAGANDA

91

GLOSSARY

authenticity has the look of being real

bias an unbalanced view of something, where one idea is promoted over alternative or opposing ideas

brand the identity of a company that is known for producing a certain kind of product

bulletin a short news broadcast

candidate the person standing for selection—or election

censorship controlling news and other media by forcing journalists to remove parts of a story—or all of it

editorial relating to the decisions about what to say and how to say it during the preparation of material for news stories

fiction literature that is a made-up story about something that never happened

fourth estate a term that refers to the people who work in journalism, and especially the owners of newspapers and TV channels

freedom of speech the right of every person on Earth to say what they think about a topic. However, that right does not automatically give the person protection from the consequences of what they say.

guerrilla a fighter who is part of a small force that attacks without warning or in an irregular way

headline the title for a news story that is meant to encourage a reader to take a closer look at the information

journal a publication that is produced regularly to publicize new discoveries made in science and other fields of research

legend a myth that is said to have taken place in history but isn't authenticated

medieval referring to the Middle Ages of Europe, generally said to be between the years 500 and 1500 CE

myth a fictional account of a very significant event in the ancient history of a country or culture

parody a type of comedy that makes fun of real things by exaggerating their characteristics

perspective a way of recording an image that reflects the three-dimensional view created by human vision, where distant objects appear smaller than those nearer to the viewer

populism an area of politics where politicians appeal to voters by turning them against the current government, saying that a few powerful people really control the country, not the ordinary people

postmodernism a school of thought saying that information does not have to produce a single true answer

PR short for "public relations," where people aim to promote and protect the public image of people and companies

press, the a general name for the news media, especially referring to the journalists that write newspapers

propaganda a way of promoting a political idea—often the deeds of a leader and government of a country—by controlling the news, including by adding fake stories and censoring bad news

psychologist a scientist that investigates the mental activity of the human mind

splash, the another name for the main story on the front page of the newspaper

web 2.0 a change in the way the internet was used to make money, by the creation of web platforms for users to store, create, and share their own content

FIND OUT MORE

Now over to you. Use these resources to continue your investigation of fake news. You can find out more in books, films, and on websites. Most importantly, though, read the papers—as many as possible! You may not always like what you read, or think it is a fair reflection of events, but reading widely will help you understand people with different opinions from you. Fake news thrives whenever there is no proper discussion of a topic in the public sphere. Instead of just saying what we think—or clicking "like" buttons—we need to have more conversations (but not arguments) with people who see things differently. Good luck!

BOOKS

There aren't many books for young people on fake news yet, but these books will give you more context on politics and the online world in which fake news exists.

Politics for Beginners, by Louie Stowell, Usborne, 2018

Dr. Christian's Guide to Growing up Online, by Dr. Christian Jessen, Scholastic, 2018

WEBSITES AND ONLINE ARTICLES

There are plenty of reliable news sources online and some websites will help you identify the fakes!

Fake News: What is it? And how to spot it, BBC Newsround
www.bbc.co.uk/newsround/38906931

Snopes, a fact checking website where you can verify stories you find online
www.snopes.com

MUSEUMS

Museums are great places to visit and discover more about the history of journalism and the web.

The International Spy Museum, Washington D.C., USA

The Museum of Broacase History, Chicago, Illinois, USA

PODCASTS

Listen to people dissect the news and cut through the lies with these podcasts.

The BBC Academy Podcast: The Truth About Fake News
A podcast providing insights into journalism and media. This episode discusses fake news and its impact.

GAMES

Put your skills to the test! See if you can spot fake news or how well you can judge sources to post your own accurate stories.

BBC iReporter lets you cover breaking news and judges how well you balance accuracy, impact, and speed!
www.bbc.co.uk/news/resources/idt-8760dd58-84f9-4c98-ade2-590562670096

Decide if these stories are true or false and learn skills to verify stories.
https://newsliteracy.ca/fakeout/

All web addresses were correct at the time of printing. The publishers and author cannot be held responsible for the content of the websites, podcasts, and apps referred to in this book.

 A FEW FINAL QUESTIONS...

Is the idea of fake news actually fake news itself? Who benefits most from the idea of fake news?

Should reporting fake news be against the law with journalists and editors being punished? What if they make a mistake? And how can you tell the difference between deliberate faking or mistaken reporting?

Should news be part of social media or made a separate service?

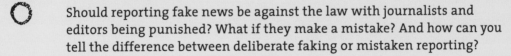

INDEX